Sylvia
Plath
in Devon
A Year's Turning

Sylvia Plath
in Devon
A Year's Turning

ELIZABETH SIGMUND
AND GAIL CROWTHER

With an Introduction by Peter K. Steinberg

FONTHILL

Fonthill Media Limited
Fonthill Media LLC
www.fonthillmedia.com
office@fonthillmedia.com

First published in the United Kingdom
and the United States of America 2014

British Library Cataloguing in Publication Data:
A catalogue record for this book is available from the British Library

ISBN 978-1-78155-437-1

Typeset in 11pt on 13pt Sabon
Printed and bound by CPI Group (UK) Ltd, Croydon, CR0 4YY

'O *may my heart's truth*
Still be sung
On this high hill in a year's turning.'

From 'Poem in October' by Dylan Thomas

Contents

Acknowledgements

I would like to thank Ronald Hayman and my husband William for their practical help, Peter K. Steinberg for his advice and friendship, Fay Weldon, Al Alvarez, and Austin Wormleighton for their sympathetic support and encouragement, Gail Crowther, who has become a wonderful friend, and Sam Jordison, without whom this book may never have appeared.

Elizabeth Sigmund

I would like to thank Peter K. Steinberg for his friendship, his excellent scholarship, archival skills, sharing of letters, drafts and data, and for being my eyes in the Lilly Library. I would also like to thank Elizabeth and William Sigmund who have been a pleasure to work with, Karen V. Kukil and Barbara Blumenthal at The Mortimer Rare Book Room, Smith College, The Rare Manuscript Reading Room at The British Library, Carl Rollyson, Vanessa Lindgren, Carolyn King, Andrew Leverton Tony Cockayne, David Fitzwilliam, Carol and Ces Crowther, Joanne and Peter Whiteside, Rob Sanders, Nicola Ashton, Jasper Hadman at Fonthill Media, and finally, my constant research and writing companion, George.

Gail Crowther

Introduction

Writing Life

Peter K. Steinberg

In *Sylvia Plath in Devon: A Year's Turning*, Elizabeth Sigmund and Gail Crowther explore Sigmund's friendship with Plath and how Plath's life in Devon influenced her work between September 1961 and December 1962. In addition to Sigmund's personal memories, the authors call on material from traditional archives and the 'living archive' to bring Plath's life and writing into sharp, clear focus, almost erasing the fact that she died more than fifty years ago.

For years, critics have called for a separation of Plath's creative writing and her popular image as a depressive figure. But Plath's life is central to her writing: she herself said that her poetry comes 'out of the sensuous and emotional experiences' and that 'personal experience is very important' (Orr, 1966: 169).

The subjects that Plath wrote about in North Tawton, the small town in Devon where she lived briefly, range widely. They include, among others, beekeeping, Thalidomide, yew trees, the experience of childbirth, the delirium caused by high fevers, a cut thumb, marital relations, poppies, and horseback riding. While each of these topics, and more, were informed by her personal experiences, Plath shapes them to have universal interest. 'Cut', for example, deals with the near amputation of her own thumb, but brings in historic themes such as the colonization of North America and the Revolutionary War against Great Britain. And further layers to this poem are revealed upon reading Plath's letters. On 9 November 1961, Plath wrote to her mother that she had ordered a carpet sample coloured turkey-red (this detail was removed when the letter appeared in *Letters Home* in 1988) for her study in Court Green, her house in North Tawton. Choosing such a bold, strong colour for her study proved comforting and inspirational to her, and the colour red appears frequently in her poetry. In 'Cut', the knowledge of these biographical particulars gives a deeper significance to the image, 'Your turkey wattle / Carpet rolls / Straight from the heart' (Plath, 1982: 235).

Shutting the door on Plath's life and the way it informed her writing flies in the face of her own stated beliefs. Her journals record dozens of instructions—credos, if you will—about her writing and the drawing of material from her life. Plath brought these credos into public view in her October 1962 interview with Peter Orr, when she related that 'personal experience is very important' to her. But she was not only concerned about herself. She commented in a 1962 *London Magazine* essay entitled 'Context' that the 'real issues' of her time 'are the issues of every time— the hurt and wonder of loving; making in all its forms—children, loaves of bread, paintings, buildings; and the conservation of life of all people in all places' (Plath, 1962: 46). Plath saw both her position as a writer and the role of poetry in the world clearly. She expertly translated these experiences, emotions, and themes into a language that is still relevant today. This is how our generation is able to understand them. Her poetry and prose has the power to transcend its personal genesis, and apply to 'the issues of every time' and still be 'relevant to the larger things, the bigger things' (Orr, 1966: 170).

In *Sylvia Plath in Devon: A Year's Turning*, Elizabeth Sigmund, an intimate friend of Plath's, recalls her unique, personal memories of their friendship. In addition to these memories, she and her co-author, Gail Crowther, allow Plath to define herself through her own correspondence, poetry, and personal papers, while adding context to Plath's life in North Tawton and the southwest of England. The result is an intimate account of this crucial period in the poet's life, which enriches both aspects of her legacy: her writing and her life.

Sigmund draws on her personal memories of her friend with care and love. Given their very different backgrounds and upbringings in England and the United States, some might find it remarkable that a deep bond was immediately established between them upon their meeting in the spring of 1962. It was the start of a period of renewed activity for Plath, following the birth of her second child, in which she would write some of her most memorable poetry. She took great notice of her surroundings and kept detailed dossier notes on her North Tawton neighbours; Elizabeth Sigmund seems to have escaped this level of documentation, which I think suggests how close she was to her new friend.

Coincidences abound with Sylvia Plath. In recollecting her own past, Sigmund reveals how unknowingly connected she and Plath were, and how, in trying to keep Plath's memory alive and fresh, she made remarkable discoveries that link them closer together. Plath built solid friendships with a small, diverse group of women and the evidence strongly suggests that had she not died, Plath and Sigmund would both have been politically and socially *committed* women.

Sylvia Plath's time in Devon was bookended by the promise of bright, sunny days. This book illustrates the hopes Plath had when moving from London—a city in which she thrived culturally and professionally—to the countryside in Devon, where she fully entrenched herself in making a comfortable, sustaining home. Much happened in that time that previous biographical coverage has either ignored or failed to recognize as important, or to which there has been limited access or knowledge of materials. But even so, her time in Devon has come under close scrutiny in biographies, and without a doubt, 1962 is one of the most important years in Plath's life. The poetry she wrote, particularly towards the end of her days in North Tawton in October 1962, is of legendary importance to twentieth-century literature. Sigmund's personal exploration of her life and creative writing in this period is remarkable given the lack of crucial primary source material, such as her final journals, letters, and novel(s).

Readers of Gail Crowther's chapter will find a careful and microscopic reconstruction of Plath's life, drawing on existing and newly uncovered archival documents, including letters to her family and friends, her poetry and prose, and her Letts Diary Tablet. Importantly, Crowther also examines the 'living archive': the physical landscapes, places and spaces in which Plath inhabited.

From her detailed analysis of the documents contained in the archives of libraries in England and the United States, Crowther reshapes our understanding of Plath's activities. From the 'living archive', she enables us to enter the spaces Plath once occupied. Crowther's visits to the places that Plath lived has given her a unique perspective on all the surviving texts that Plath produced there. It is this first-hand experience that informs the concept of the living archive, offering 'a blueprint for the production of a text. Thus when the living archive is re-visited, there is a chance that some of that original blueprint will still be in place' (Crowther and Steinberg, 2013: 38). Through this journey, Crowther discusses Plath's poetry and prose and identifies her inspiration from real life, highlighting the control and mastery of Plath's craft. Crowther rightly acknowledges that assuming Plath's work is entirely autobiographical and reading it solely from that perspective can be problematic. However, to deny the link between Plath's own life and experiences and her poetical subjects and output goes directly against her own repeatedly stated practices and beliefs.

Plath's poetry drew from her own life. An undated journal entry from 1950 spells this out quite clearly: 'my happiness streams from having wrenched a piece out of my life, a piece of hurt and beauty, and transformed it to typewritten words on paper' (2000: 22). These authorial philosophies can be found throughout her journals and remind us that her experiences are a launch pad to deeper meaning. The spark of inspiration was life-based, but Plath's art runs much deeper. In this transformation of personal experience to words, Plath elevated private experience into the universal, creating wider social and political meaning from individual emotions.

In this book's beautiful appendix, 'A Poem, A Friend', Sigmund and Crowther investigate the unconscious sources of Sigmund's poem 'Shep-en-Mut'. Here, the reader is invited to 'explore words, memories and stories as we follow the labyrinthine path of poems, people, and play'. The poem and the story of its genesis explore Sigmund's friendship with Plath, the flexibility of interpretation, and the spark of poetry whereby the uncanny and the unfamiliar are brought together.

Finally, a little personal back-story. I met Gail via email in July 2007 when she was working on her PhD thesis *The Haunted Reader and Sylvia Plath*, and a few months later in person at the Sylvia Plath 75th Year Symposium in Oxford. In the winter of 2008-09, I made Elizabeth's acquaintance after being interviewed by Alison Flood in *The Guardian* about the staging of Plath's poem, 'Three Women'. I then introduced Elizabeth and Gail, and they developed a friendship similar to the one Elizabeth had developed with Plath. It was first through letters (emails), then phone conversations, and ultimately in person. The resulting friendship between the three of us has passed the length of time in which Elizabeth knew Plath, and I can only imagine how deep a bond these two women would have developed had things been different. Elizabeth and I maintained a telephone-only relationship until March 2013, when Gail, Elizabeth, and I met together for the first time at Plymouth University, where Gail and I were presenting a paper on Plath and her archives. For me, it was the highlight of my years spent researching Sylvia Plath. That evening, over tea and cake in Elizabeth's house, I recognized in Elizabeth's friendly eyes and demeanour the warmth which Plath felt in Devon more than half a century earlier, in March 1962.

Plath wrote movingly on the reach of poetry:

> I am not worried that poems reach relatively few people. As it is, they go surprisingly far—among strangers, around the world, even. Farther than the words of a classroom teacher or the prescriptions of a doctor; if they are very lucky, farther than a lifetime.
>
> (Plath, 1962: 46)

Sylvia Plath is a connective figure. Her poetry, prose and other writing is read and beloved around the world, giving each of her reader's special messages and comfort. In contrast to the negativity that has plagued her reputation since her death, Plath's work is a great source of pleasure, happiness, and strength to many. *Sylvia Plath in Devon: A Year's Turning* resuscitates Plath's vivacity and her love of life, of writing, and of people. Like the above quote states, Plath—her poetry and her person—has gone 'surprisingly far—among strangers, around the world, even.'

Peter K. Steinberg
Boston, Massachusetts
November 2013

Chapter 1

Sylvia in Devon

Elizabeth Sigmund

Several people have asked me to write about my friendship with Sylvia Plath. I knew her very well in the last year of her life, and I feel that it is appropriate to describe my own background, as it is perhaps unusual. I am not a biographer, an academic or a journalist, and can only write as Sylvia's friend, but I have read many of the books about her and Ted, sometimes with dismay.

I was born in 1928 in Lancashire. My mother was one of twelve children, my grandmother was a Garnett, related to David Garnett, and my grandfather owned two cotton-bleaching mills and was a colonel in the First World War. When I was four years old my father left us to join Oswald Mosley's Blackshirts, and so my mother and I went back to live with my maternal grandparents, in a big house on the edge of the moors.

I was a lonely child as I didn't go to school until I was eleven; my mother taught me, and then I had a governess. I could read when I was four, and went through all the classic English children's books. My youngest uncle was a brilliant pianist, and I fell asleep many times hearing him play Beethoven, Chopin and Bach. This has left me with a passionate love of literature and music. When I was nine, someone asked me what I wanted to be when I grew up. I replied, 'An opera singer!'

I spent a lot of time wandering about our vast garden, dreaming of *The Secret Garden*. My cousins used to visit occasionally, but I always felt an outsider. I went to Bolton Grammar School when I was eleven and we had moved into a town house, which for the first time gave me a taste of social life with my own generation.

Nothing could be more different than this history from Sylvia's, with her brilliant academic brain, and her mother's ambition for her. However, I think that she found the contrast fascinating, and as I didn't fall into any of the categories of most of her associates—either having designs on Ted, or intellectual competitors—I think she felt at ease with me.

When I first met Sylvia in March 1962, she was twenty-nine and I was thirty-three, married to a writer, David Compton. It was almost a year before she died. Her daughter Frieda was almost two years old, my son James was three years old, and Sylvia's son Nicholas was a month old. Sylvia and Ted had bought Court Green, a beautiful seventeenth-century thatched house in North Tawton, a tiny mill town near Okehampton on the edge of Dartmoor.

I had made contact with them a year earlier after hearing them speaking on a Radio 3 programme called *Two of a Kind*, in which they described

Elizabeth Sigmund, Cornwall, 1988. (*Elizabeth Sigmund*)

living in a tiny flat in London, where they had to write in turns, with their writing boards balanced on the edge of their baby daughter's playpen. We were then living in a big thatched farmhouse in a village called Fairy Cross in North Devon. I suggested that they might like to spend a holiday with us. I could look after Frieda with our three children, and carry out all the domestic chores, while they could write in peace. After a year's silence I had forgotten the offer, but suddenly I had a letter from Ted saying that they, too, were living in an old thatched house not twenty miles away and would love to see us.

My first impression of Sylvia was of a tall, slim, vividly alive young woman, with waist-length brown hair. During this visit and further visits throughout the spring, she took me round the house and garden, describing her plans for a family of five children, the vegetables she was growing, the honey her bees were going to produce, and the wonderful poetry Ted would write. She showed me the mound (known as a 'tump' by local people) in the orchard, which, she had been told, was possibly a bronze-age burial site. Subsequently, Ted had a writing-hut built on top of it. Much later I discovered that it was the remains of a Norman motte and bailey.

Sylvia was excited when she learnt that I worked with the local Liberal Party, and rushed to Ted to say 'I have found a committed woman', which I found very funny. I introduced her to Mark Bonham Carter, the prospective Liberal parliamentary candidate for mid-Devon, and they became close friends. She and I discussed the military and industrial links between Britain and the US, and she was very pleased that we agreed on so many political points. I read in a biography, written after her death, that Sylvia had gone to see the first CND march from Aldermaston arrive in Trafalgar Square. We also had other interests in common—the teachings of C. G. Jung and the paediatric specialist, Dr Spock.

We planned visits, and she became enamoured with the 'earth mother' image she had given me. We had by now moved into a mill-house in North Devon, with no electricity, three children to bring up, and very little money. She later wrote to me, 'You must never leave your house, I see you always with your little twinkly lights.' She meant our candles and smoky oil lamps!

Sylvia was fascinated by other peoples' lives and told me of her home help's husband, who combined the roles of bell-ringer, fireman and amateur undertaker in North Tawton. In the latter role he was employed to wheel the coffin on a trolley to the funeral, for people too poor to afford a hearse. The people in the village grew used to her friendly American ways, and many were heart-broken by her death. She told me that she had never felt so at home before. She gave poetry readings for an arts group in Okehampton, a market town on the edge of the moor. She helped them to raise the money to buy an old building for an arts centre for the district, and they told me how fond they had become of her.

Over the spring and summer we visited each other regularly, each delighting in having found a friend in Devon with so many things in common. She repeatedly spoke of Ted's wonderful poetry and said that she was typing it and submitting it to various journals.

On 6 July 1962, Sylvia and Ted came to my thirty-fourth birthday party. She brought a beautiful home-made iced cake with thirty-five candles on it. 'One to grow on,' she said. Sylvia enchanted my other guests with her friendliness and wit. After Sylvia's death, one of them wrote of this in a letter to the *Times Literary Supplement*, which elicited a furious response from Ted's sister, Olwyn.

The impression of Ted and Sylvia as a unit, a couple who hardly needed words in order to communicate, was unassailable. I have this image of them leaning side by side over our bridge, gazing into the peaty trout stream with utter concentration. Their life was something so rare and different from anything I had come across before, and I knew that Sylvia depended on it so profoundly that it was impossible to imagine her life without it.

I had no idea that there was any discord in their lives, except that Sylvia told me that she had some concerns about the visit her mother, Aurelia, had planned for July. I knew that her relationship with Aurelia was strained, as I too had a mother whose husband had left her when I was a small child. Sylvia's father had, of course, died, and we both felt a burden of responsibility for our mother's well-being, which could be painful. She did not tell me of a visit they had had from a couple, David and Assia Wevill, and I was not aware of any anxiety she felt about Assia's relationship with Ted.

So I was intensely shocked when, three days after my birthday in July, Sylvia arrived in her car with Nick in his carry-cot. She wept and gripped my hands, saying, 'Ted lies to me. He lies. He is having an affair and he has become a little man.' She said that she couldn't feed Nick: 'My milk has dried up.' She told me that their friend, Assia Wevill, had telephoned to speak to Ted, assuming a man's deep voice, and when Ted came to answer the call, Sylvia waited until the call was over and then pulled the plug out of the wall. She challenged Ted with the stupidity of the attempted deception, and it was clear from his demeanour that her suspicion was true. She stayed the night with us, and I knew that the breaking of this intense and powerful relationship could only cause great damage.

Ted went to stay with friends in London, and during that sad autumn, when Sylvia was living at Court Green without Ted, she came to visit more often. She brought fruit, vegetables and honey from her garden. We had long discussions about her sense of loss and anger, but I had no idea of the amazing poetry that she was writing early every morning.

In September, Sylvia came to see us full of hope and excitement, saying that she and Ted were going to stay in Ireland. Ireland had always represented nirvana for them, and she obviously thought that this was a rapprochement. However, ten days later, she came to see us again, bone-thin and smoking (something she had always found repellent), and told me that Ted had left in the middle of the third night in Connemara—without leaving a message or any indication of why or where he was going. This second rejection was devastating. I have recently learnt that he had planned this in detail, having asked a friend in London to post a series of cards to her, and having previously arranged to join Assia in Spain.

We tried to cheer Sylvia with various outings. One was to a concert of early baroque music; she was amazed at the raw rich sound, but most of all by the strange names of the instruments—viola da gamba, rebeq, bowed psaltery, etc.

After the second desertion, Sylvia became determined to move to London—she told me that she had found the perfect place, a flat in a house where Yeats had lived. I had great anxiety over the thought of her leaving Court Green (although, as she later wrote to me, it was only going to be until the spring), and about her being in London, where the 'other woman', Assia Wevill, was living with Ted.

Sylvia wrote a series of letters to me during this period, and in one of them she said that Ted came to visit the children: 'I can't help sighing for lost Edens.' She wrote of the bitter cold and that she had no heating. She was suffering from flu and sinusitis.

Her last letter to me, which I received six days before she died, was full of plans. In it she said that she had found a nursery school for Frieda, that she was having Nick's 'wandery' eye fixed, and that she had been invited to compere a poetry-reading at the Round House and to join 'The Critics', a prestigious Radio 3 programme. She said that she would be back at Court Green to see her daffodils: 'Thank God you will be there.' She also told us that she had dedicated *The Bell Jar* to us, and said that we appeared in her new novel about life in North Tawton as plaster saints. Not flattering, I fear. This novel, *Double Exposure*, along with journals and other things, disappeared after her death.

The first edition of *The Bell Jar* was published by Heinemann under the *nom de plume* Victoria Lucas. It carried the dedication 'for Elizabeth and David' on the page facing the first chapter. Some years later a friend pointed out that the second edition, published by Faber and Faber, carried no dedication. I wrote to the *Times Literary Supplement* saying how sad I was that this had been cut out, and asked why it had happened. I received a complete apology from Charles Monteith, the editor at Faber and Faber, saying that they hadn't noticed it. Another explanation came in a personal letter from Olwyn Hughes to me, saying that Faber and Faber must have been trying to save paper!

Al Alvarez's article *A Poet's Epitaph* was published on 17 February 1963 in the *Observer*. I do not need to describe the grief and sense of horror I felt. To see the photograph of Sylvia and little Frieda below such terrible words was unbearable. I telephoned Alvarez, and all I remember is us both crying, and saying, 'It's too terrible—such a waste.' We had both thought that she had been coming to terms with her situation and couldn't understand what had pushed her over the edge. I later learnt of two possible causes.

In one of Sylvia's last visits to us before she went to stay in London, she had said, 'If anything happens to me please promise that you will stay close to the children.' At the time I took this as an over-dramatic request. Now I had to face it as a fact.

A few weeks after Sylvia died, I went to London to visit Ted and the children at Fitzroy Road. The nanny told me that Assia was living there, and that day she was having an abortion. When they came back from the hospital, Ted gave me *The Bell Jar,* and said that he could hear the wolves howling in the zoo (Regent's Park is nearby): 'Somehow it seems appropriate.' He looked distraught. Nick was silent and the nanny said that he wouldn't eat and would only drink milk.

If Sylvia had known of Assia's pregnancy it would have been a terrible shock. One of the aspects of Sylvia's poems about Assia was of her inability to bear children: 'A marble womb where no fish swims.'

When I later learnt that the BBC had broadcast Ted's play *The Difficulties of a Bridegroom* twice in the weeks leading up to her death, I felt that this also could have added to her feeling of despair and humiliation. This play has nothing to do with the short story of this name which he wrote later. The plot of the play concerns a married man driving to London to see his mistress; he runs over and kills a hare. (Ted told Sylvia that the hare was her shamanic mystical animal). He takes the hare to a butcher and buys red roses for his mistress with the money. The play describes a strange mixture of fascination with, and revulsion towards, his mistress's body.

Ted wrote to me soon after my visit, asking us to go and live at Court Green. He said that he couldn't bear to go back: 'The house is full of ghosts. I must sell it.' He asked if we would act as caretakers, and show possible buyers round. We agreed, after much thought. It was a painful decision, but one which seemed the only way in which we could help in this agonising situation. One of the most painful things about moving into Court Green was the discovery of a line of Sylvia's shoes in the bathroom. Shoes are so personal, and there was something horribly final about their presence.

The people in North Tawton were very shocked at Sylvia's death, and many stopped, in tears, to talk to me to say what a lovely young woman she was.

While living at Court Green I discovered two extraordinary coincidences linking my life with Sylvia's. The first was that Sylvia's beloved midwife, Winifred Davies, was my mother's cousin. Born Winifred Garnett, she was a member of the Yorkshire branch of the family, and my maternal grandmother was her aunt and second cousin of the writer David Garnett. The second surprise was that I found a poem dedicated to Sylvia by Peter

Davison, then editor of *Atlantic Monthly*. She had had a brief affair with him in Cambridge, Massachusetts, in 1955, and I had had an equally brief affair with him in Cambridge, England, in 1949. We both appear in his autobiography *Half Remembered*, published in 1973 by Harper and Row. Sylvia would have been amazed and delighted by these coincidences, but not surprised.

Shortly after we moved into Court Green, Ted called to say that he was coming down to collect some things for the London flat. Assia had decided to accompany him. She knew of our affection for Sylvia, and after an uncomfortable lunch she told Ted to ask me to show her round the house. I knew that she had been to stay there while Sylvia was alive. When we reached Sylvia's padlocked workroom, Assia said, 'Don't you feel a traitor?' I said that I did and wouldn't go any further. While I was helping Ted tie up a carpet, Assia came into the room, and after observing that Ted was in tears she said to me, 'Do you think that Ted and I can be happy?' I said, 'No. Sylvia will always be between you.' She burst into hysterical tears and Ted bundled her into the car and drove off.

Some weeks later, Assia sent me the North Thames gas bill for Sylvia's flat for the period when Sylvia gassed herself, with a note saying, 'I believe this covers your occupation of Court Green.' I opened it and saw that this was the period when Sylvia had died. When Ted rang up, I told him. 'Oh, stupid girl,' he said, 'she does get in a muddle.'

In one of Ted's letters to us he said, 'The difficulties are odd and several. When I live with the children they become utterly obsessed with me, Frieda especially, and my presence is a permanent reminder that somebody is missing. I could live with Nick alone, because he's self-sufficient and remembers nothing, but Frieda is complicated—she seems to sense everything. The minute I'm alone with her, or with her and Nick, she enters into a sort of conspiracy of mourning with me. This must be my fault for showing something or not being ebullient enough.' Later in this same letter he says, 'When somebody who has shared life with you as much as Sylvia shared it with me dies then life somehow dies, the gold standard of it is somehow converted into death and it is a minute by minute effort to find any sense in life, or any value.' A number of letters to us from Ted, and several from Aurelia Plath, are in the British Library.

Ted told me that he had had Sylvia's body embalmed, and when I found that she had been buried in Heptonstall, in Yorkshire, I was very sad. She had loved her 'wall of dead', the wall of the churchyard in North Tawton which looked directly down through the orchard to the front of her beloved house. This seemed the appropriate place for her to be buried. She had told me that she found Yorkshire cold and forbidding.

In the months after Sylvia's death, Ted appointed his sister Olwyn as Sylvia's literary agent, and there followed various publications which were carefully angled to paint a picture of Ted as an innocent victim of Sylvia's alleged neurotic possessiveness and jealousy. Olwyn wrote a letter to Sylvia's and my late friend Clarissa Roche, saying of Sylvia, 'I know you liked her—I found her straight poison. God preserve me from mixed-up kids.' This so-called mixed-up kid earned Olwyn a great deal of money. In 2013, Olwyn was interviewed by Sam Jordison for *The Guardian* Reading Group's discussion of *The Bell Jar*, and while discussing Plath's behaviour, Olwyn referred to her as a 'monster'.

Ted and Olwyn had, by now, complete control not only over Sylvia's work, but also over her history. When Alvarez wrote two pieces for *The Observer*, Ted had the second part rejected. When a critical opinion of *Bitter Fame*, a biography of Sylvia written by Anne Stevenson, was discussed on the BBC, Ted threatened to sue. At the same time he wrote to the *Western Morning News* saying, 'I do not approve of the book, and dissociate myself from any responsibility for the opinions and conclusions contained in it.'

Stevenson's book received a number of severely critical reviews, and it was clearly regarded as jointly written by Olwyn and Anne Stevenson. This resulted in a savage cartoon in *Private Eye* portraying Ted as a stage magician, pulling a rabbit out of a hat, while his sister Olwyn, as his assistant, was sticking knives into Sylvia's corpse, lying in a coffin.

When Anne Stevenson came to Exeter University in 1989 to speak about the book, Clarissa Roche and I joined the audience. When I had given my name, I attempted to ask Anne a question but the chairwoman refused to let me speak. Many of my friends were there and protested, saying, 'She actually knew Sylvia, let her speak.' Ted's second wife, Carol Hughes, sat at the back of the audience, tape recording the proceedings. I wonder why.

After Ted and the children came back to live at Court Green, we bought an old thatched cottage nearby and I was determined to maintain close links with them. This was because of Nick and Frieda, but also because no-one else in the literary circle who gathered around them had known Sylvia, and she was never mentioned. I wished to be a link between Sylvia and the children, but also between Sylvia and Ted. He knew this, and there grew a strange tacit relationship between us in which he knew that I loved Sylvia, but would never do anything to hurt him or the children. If he had decided that silence and forgetfulness was the only safe way to exist, then I would abide by it, which I did, until the books and articles began to appear portraying Sylvia as a depressive neurotic and incapable of giving love.

In 1976, Alvarez asked me to write a memoir of Sylvia for *The New Review*, and I agreed. First I had to ask Ted's opinion of this project. He said, 'The time to tell the truth about Sylvia is when you're dying.' I wondered whose truth he meant, and determined to go ahead. The piece was very moderate and accused Ted of nothing, but I was subsequently told by Olwyn that I would not be allowed to see the children again, and indeed I did not, until the day of Ted's funeral in North Tawton on 3 November 1998, when they took the front of Ted's coffin to carry it out of the church to the hearse.

In 1990, Ted sued Trevor Thomas, the half-blind old professor of fine art who had lived in the flat below Sylvia in Fitzroy Road. Professor Thomas had written and circulated a memoir of his experiences of Sylvia and Ted, and had been in fact the last person to see Sylvia alive, and to talk with her. He was obliged to apologise for and withdraw his memoir. I still have a copy.

Over the years, journalists and biographers have interviewed me, and when I have tried to convey my impression of Sylvia I have been accused of being a rabid feminist, a liar, a self-publicist and jealous because Ted did not have a sexual relationship with me. I knew the risk I was taking of attracting these attacks, but the most difficult was the accusation, which still persists, of hurting Frieda and Ted's second wife Carol by saying anything.

I cannot forget Ted's words to me in the last communication I had with him. Soon after Sylvia had died, Ted gave me a copy of Dylan Thomas's *The Collected Poems*, in which she had marked many passages, including Thomas's note:

... These poems, with all their crudities, doubts and confusions, are written for the love of Man and in praise of God, and I'd be a damn' fool if they weren't.

The message she marked most strongly were the last lines of 'Poem in October':

O may my heart's truth
Still be sung
On this high hill in a year's turning.

Such a desperate cry, and one which leaves a responsibility which must be weighed against the fear of being accused of making use of others' sufferings to gain notoriety. I must leave the judgement to others. Alvarez said, 'You must do what you believe to be right, and what you feel that Sylvia would have wanted.'

This is that attempt.

Elizabeth Sigmund
April 2013

Chapter 2

Sylvia Plath in Devon
31 August 1961—10 December 1962

Gail Crowther

OL: How much room have you got to live in?
SP: Oh not enough. We have a very small flat—a bedroom, a sitting room, a kitchen and a bath, which is—has a rather juggling affair when it comes to managing a nine month old baby, and we're—we're dreaming of a house where I can shout to Ted from one end to the other and he won't be able to hear me, but I don't know how far away that is.

> Sylvia Plath interviewed by Owen Leeming for *Poets in Partnership*, 18 January 1961.

At last I have all the room I could want and a perfect place for everything.

> Letter from Sylvia Plath to Aurelia Plath, 4 September 1961.

Places are important.

The spaces in which we choose to live, work, love and daydream leave their traces on us as much as we imbue places with our memories and actions. Once a space has been touched by us it loses its neutrality and becomes part of our landscape long after we have gone. Sylvia Plath spent just over a year living in North Tawton, Devon, and today for Plath's readers, the location where she composed some of her most brilliant poems remains a place of fascination; her words and presence are seemingly suspended in that landscape, imprinted, immoveable. Much has been written about Plath during this time, often with a focus on the breakdown of her marriage to Ted Hughes and the extraordinary outburst of the *Ariel* poems that, in Plath's own words, would 'make her name'. What has often been overlooked are other aspects of Plath's time in Devon; her immersion into local town life, her love of gardening and growing vegetables, learning horse riding and forging new friendships. While undoubtedly Plath suffered distress during this year, she arrived in (and left) Devon full of hope. She grew to love her large country house and two-acre garden with the sprawl and hump of Dartmoor round about. It was the space that she loved — the openness, the wide skies and the clear air of a spring day.

Following her marriage in 1956, living space for Plath had been in short supply. She and Hughes occupied a series of rented flats and apartments on both sides of the Atlantic, which always consisted of one bedroom and a small living area. When Plath gave the interview (above) to Owen Leeming for the BBC in January 1961, she was living with Hughes and their daughter, Frieda, in a small, one-bedroom apartment in Chalcot Square, Primrose Hill, London. The apartment had been newly refurbished and Plath chose white and vermillion painted walls, black and brown prints for the bathroom, and creamy wallpaper with red and pink roses for her bedroom. Sample swatches of this paper which Plath sent to her mother, Aurelia Plath, still sit in the archives of Lilly Library at Indiana University, their vibrancy unfaded.

It is interesting to ponder what happened to these places, these small apartments filled with chairs and tables, beds and cupboards. Today, the Chalcot Square flat remains almost the same with its slightly tilting floor and the creaking floorboards. In places, Plath's vermillion red paint is still visible. When an English Heritage blue plaque was erected here by her children Frieda and Nicholas Hughes commemorating Plath in 2000, Frieda expressed her astonishment at the small space in which she had lived with her parents. Similarly across the Atlantic, the apartment in which Plath and Hughes lived during the year she taught English at Smith College (1957–1958) was described by Aurelia Plath as cramped and small. As with Chalcot Square, today this flat remains virtually unchanged. In 2012, 337 Elm Street in Northampton, Massachusetts, was listed for sale. Inside the apartment, ghostly vestiges of the past were even more apparent. Odd bits of furniture were lying around which had been there for decades, unchanged. A vintage *Bissell's Vanity* carpet sweeper, an old General Electric refrigerator, two red and mustard coloured cases in the living room closet. In the bedroom alcove stood a pale wooden dresser, six drawers in total, three drawers high, with silver handles and a mirror. Plath described this very dresser in her journal, 'A fake white-wood bureau three drawers high, with a bright gild handle on every drawer, juts out of the alcove...' (2000: 314). A curious relic, still standing in place for fifty-six years bearing the traces of former inhabitants. 'Rooms,' wrote Plath, 'Every room a world' (2000: 306). The rooms in which Plath lived over the years until she moved to Devon were tiny, yet each room held a story, stamped with an indelible watermark of her life.

The move to Devon, for Sylvia Plath, signified the end of an adult life living in cramped spaces. It was also a significant and startling time in Plath's life as a whole, for in just a year's turning, she created a home from a crumbling manor house, gave birth to her son, settled into village life, and experienced the end of her marriage. Professionally, she saw her poetry collection *The Colossus* published in America, oversaw the publication of her first novel *The Bell Jar*, and wrote her blistering *Ariel* poems before beginning provisional work on a second novel entitled *Double Exposure*.

Prior to her move to Devon, the 1961 Owen Leeming interview with Plath and Hughes featured as part of a BBC series called *Two of a Kind: Poets in Partnership*. Recorded on 18 January, 1961 and broadcast almost two weeks later on the 31st, this interview was the first time that Elizabeth Sigmund, then living in an old farmhouse in Fairy Cross, Devon had heard of the writer, Sylvia Plath.[1] As the wife of a writer herself, Sigmund sympathised with the lack of productive working space and wrote to Plath and Hughes via the BBC inviting them to stay with her. Although her letter remained unanswered for over a year, it did have an impact on Plath and she wrote to her mother on 26 February informing her of this unexpected invitation.[2] When Sigmund's letter was finally acknowledged, the reply came from Ted Hughes, in Devon, inviting Elizabeth and her then husband David Compton, to afternoon tea.

Court Green, North Tawton, Devon. The house Sylvia Plath and Ted Hughes bought in August 1961. (*Peter K. Steinberg*)

Just over six months after Plath and Hughes had given the BBC interview daydreaming of a large house and much space, they had moved from London to North Tawton. Their home was Court Green, an old manor house with two and a half acres of grounds including a disused tennis court, an apple orchard, and an ancient castle *motte*. Plath felt traces of the past all over Court Green. She discovered an old, tumbled-down chicken house, a dark, windowless room off the downstairs hallway containing bottles of jam and gin belonging to former residents. Both she and Hughes delighted in the three large elms that grew near the castle *motte*, a site of supposed power and ancient history.[3] The *motte*, thirty-five metres in diameter and two metres high, was most likely a flat-topped castle mound thought to date from the twelfth century. This trace of the past appeared to make Court Green especially evocative for Plath. She wrote proudly to her mother in April 1962 that an archaeologist had been to visit the *motte* in the garden.

The house itself was a thatched manor house with white walls, black window trims and a yellow front door. The back door leading from the cobbled courtyard was a thick, ancient, wooden studded door, not unlike the one found in St Peter's Church at the end of the garden. The courtyard was laid with cobbles from the Napoleonic era, with the flat stone surface of the cobble facing upwards to prevent the mud oozing from below. The courtyard was surrounded by outbuildings—old stables, a rundown cottage, sheds and store rooms. Entering the back door, the cobbles of the courtyard ran the full length of the downstairs hall from front to back door. On the right was a large kitchen with table and chairs and an old wood-burning stove to heat water and dry clothes. It was here—the heart of the house—that meals were eaten. The first left in the hallway led to a smaller kitchen in which Plath had installed a modern sink and cooker. Here she did her cooking and washing up. Beyond this room was the laundry and pantry where Plath had installed, thanks to her mother's generosity, a Bendix washing machine. The ancient walls of the house were so thick, up to six feet in some places, that the installation of the washing machine pipes was something of a Herculean task for the workmen. The second left from the hallway (opposite the staircase on the right) was a dark cupboard for coats and brooms, and beyond this was yet more storage. Encased between the kitchen and the playroom, this was an airless, windowless area, which Plath described to Elizabeth as being 'quite frightening'. Indeed it seems likely that, over a year later when Plath was writing her poem 'Wintering', she conjured up this room in the lines:

Wintering in a dark without window
At the heart of the house . . .
This is the room I have never been in.
This is the room I could never breathe in. (1990: 218)

The final doorway on the left just before the front door led to the playroom, which Plath described as a fun room full of toys, a piano, and painted furniture. By Easter of 1962, this had a black and white checked linoleum floor, and it was in this room that Elizabeth Sigmund first met and had tea with Plath and Hughes. Opposite the playroom on the right was the living room, with bookshelves, a window seat, and a fireplace. Plath would eventually decorate this room in shades of red, with shiny copper brushes and shovels on the hearth. Both the living room and the playroom looked out across the front lawn to St Peter's Church and a large yew tree, separated from Court Green's garden by a wall of ancient headstones. This is the view that would feature in one of Plath's breakthrough poems 'The Moon and the Yew Tree' where the speaker describes how:

> Fumy, spirituous mists inhabit this place.
> Separated from my house by a row of headstones.
>
> I simply cannot see where there is to get to. (1990: 172)

Equally, over a year later, this view features again in 'Letter in November' as the speaker embraces with affection not only what she can see but the enormity of the past:

> And the wall of old corpses.
> I love them.
> I love them like history. (1990: 253)

Upstairs, directly above the playroom, Plath chose the largest room for her study. This space had two windows—one looking out across the front lawn to the church and the side window looking out across to the disused tennis court. Beneath this window, Hughes planted a peach tree. Next to this room, also at the front of the house was the children's bedroom (Frieda's brother Nicholas would be born in January 1962, almost five months after the move) and next to this was Plath and Hughes's room. The back bedroom was the guest room, which overlooked the courtyard and the three large elms near the castle *motte*. The bathroom was to the left, halfway up the staircase, and overlooked the drive up to the house and the row of four cottages. Finally, Hughes made his study in the eaves of the thatch, snugly, Plath related to her mother, over the hot water tank in the bathroom.

Moving from a one-bedroom flat in which Plath had to write in the living room and Hughes on a foldaway card table in the tiny hallway, Court Green did indeed offer Plath all the room she wanted. Yet interestingly, reactions to the house are mixed. In letters, despite the bitter cold of a winter there, Plath appeared to love Court Green unconditionally and described it as a place which lovingly responded to care. Hughes also seemed to love the house, retaining it and living there up to his death in 1998. And Elizabeth Sigmund shared this love, describing it as 'lovely and inviting, if a little creaky'. Yet Clarissa Roche, Plath's friend from America, was not taken with Court Green at all. She found it dark, cold, and somewhat creepy. During a visit in November 1962, Roche was so scared that she slept with the light on all night convinced that there was a ghost in the hallway outside the guest room. She worried about Plath living there on her own during the autumn and winter of 1962. Assia Wevill, who would later have an affair with Ted Hughes, described Court Green in a less supernatural, but equally negative, light. In her diaries and in conversation she found it primitive, 'naively' decorated, and so old that she felt sure the weeds of the courtyard grew up between the cobbles of the hallway.

Of course, how we react to a place is much dependent on the imagination we bring with us. A house is rarely just a house when it engages with our thoughts, fantasies, and emotions. For Plath and Hughes, love of Court Green could well have been influenced by the happy months they initially spent there together, planning their future, growing flowers and vegetables, and forging a new life in the country. For Elizabeth, Court Green was the site of a happy meeting with a new and stimulating friend. When Clarissa Roche visited, Plath regaled her with tales of ritualistic fire burnings, spells, and witchcraft dolls stuffed up the living room chimney, which perhaps is why her guest was left somewhat spooked. For Wevill, Court Green represented something with which she could attack Plath, the talented wife of the man with whom she was having an affair.

Ghosts can take many different forms. They do not have to be the supernatural phantoms imagined by Roche, they can simply be relics of the past that continue to haunt; traces that refuse to budge, despite the passing of time. Certainly, Carol Hughes, Ted Hughes's second wife, in a radio interview given in 2011, spoke poignantly about how long it took to reclaim Court Green as their own, despite Plath only living there for just over a year. Perhaps part of this is the immortalisation of the place in Plath's work. Anyone who has ever visited Court Green can appreciate the sensation of almost stepping into a Plath poem. The row of headstones, the gothic yew tree, the apple orchard and the courtyard. How do you reclaim a space that is suspended on the page? A text, a poem, stamps itself so vividly that it refuses to be wiped away. Plath's poems haunt Court Green and so, consequently, does her voice.

Hughes was well aware of this, and as he drafted early versions of the poems that would become *Birthday Letters*, years after Plath's death, he struggled with this aspect of her haunting. In his notebooks held in The British Library there is a draft of an undated, untitled poem in which he rages at how the ghost of Plath brings her readers to Court Green. The voice rails angrily against what he describes as 'monkeys' crawling over the yew tree and the church with cameras, peering over Plath's ghostly shoulder at the inhabitants of Court Green who are encased in her mausoleum. Certainly one detects the anguish in Hughes's voice at the inescapability of it all when he accuses Plath of inviting and enjoying every minute. So in this sense, ghosts never really go away and the past remains in the present, seemingly replaying its events *in perpetuum*.

The first time Plath and Hughes laid eyes on Court Green was the morning of 28 July, 1961. They had recently returned from just over two weeks in France. In fact the whole summer of 1961 would have professional and personal significance for Plath and is worth exploring in more detail. Plath's mother had arrived in mid-June to stay in London and meet her first grandchild, Frieda. Since the Chalcot Square flat was too small to accommodate any visitors, friends of Plath and Hughes, W. S. and Dido Merwin, offered assistance. They let Aurelia stay in their flat just around the corner at 11 St George's Terrace while they themselves spent the summer in France. When Plath and Hughes left for their holiday on 28 June, Frieda stayed with her grandmother in the Chalcot Square flat. Sailing from Dover to Boulogne, Plath and Hughes drove down the Normandy and Brittany coast stopping at places such as Berck-Plage, Douarnenez, Finisterre, the Pointe du Raz and the Pointe du Van.[4] Some of these places would be stored by Plath in her creative imagination for up to a year and then explode in some of her most powerful poems written in Devon. Plath and Hughes spent a week making their way down the country, planning to visit the Merwins in their home at Lacan de Loubressac on Wednesday 5 July. One account of this visit can be found in the appendix to *Bitter Fame*, 'Vessel of Wrath: A Memoir of Sylvia Plath', written by Dido Merwin some years later. It is certainly not the kindest account. Merwin's claim that the visit was cut short by Plath's appalling behaviour does not seem to be supported by the letters and postcards sent from Plath and Hughes. Indeed the written evidence shows that they stayed the full time they had planned, and during the visit went to local market fairs, the caves at Lascaux, and on their last night enjoyed a 'banquet' supper prepared by Dido Merwin for Jean Luçat, a French tapestry maker. By Thursday 13 July, Plath and Hughes had gone to Rouen and Mont St Michel arriving back in London in time for supper on Friday the 14th. On the 18th, they drove Aurelia Plath and Frieda up to Heptonstall in Yorkshire for a visit to meet Ted's parents, then back to London in time to head into Devon and Cornwall, house hunting.

As stated in the BBC interview earlier that year, a larger home had certainly been an aim of Plath and Hughes, and now as Hughes's fame grew, it seemed he was keen to escape the pressures of literary London and move somewhere more remote where he could concentrate solely on writing. Plath, more enamoured with city life, was reluctant to leave behind the cinemas, art galleries, and social life they had established, but in characteristic fashion, threw herself into the potential move wholeheartedly. Documents held in The British Library show that at this time Plath and Hughes were not thinking only about the West Country. Papers from 1961 contain house details sent to Hughes about homes in Crawley, Sussex. However, by the time the house hunting trip was under way on Thursday 27 July, Plath and Hughes had eight properties lined up to view—all in either Devon or Cornwall. Court Green was the third house they viewed on the 28th, and according to Aurelia Plath, they fell in love with it immediately.

It took only one month to organise buying the property. They arranged for the current owners, Lord and Lady Arundel, to treat Court Green for various death-watch beetle and woodworm infestations. Additionally, they agreed to loans from both Plath's mother and Hughes's parents, enabling them to keep their mortgage to a minimum of £600. So quickly did this happen, that by 31 August, Plath and Hughes had left their Chalcot Square flat and moved to North Tawton. As with the events of the summer, which retrospectively were so significant, other factors were also to become crucial. After advertising in *The Evening Standard*, their London flat was sublet to David and Assia Wevill, a couple who appeared to be talented and artistic. David Wevill was a struggling poet and Assia Wevill an advertising copywriter. Within eight months, Hughes and Assia Wevill would begin an affair which contributed to the unravelling of the Plath–Hughes marriage and the end of their life together in Court Green.

An eerie time-twist poem, 'The Pan', in Hughes's *Birthday Letters*, describes this future awaiting them. It begins the day he and Plath moved from London to North Tawton. Arriving at five in the afternoon, they drive down the main street and stop to buy a pan to heat milk and food for the baby. Hughes does not notice that the shop where he buys the pan has already been closed for two years, or his future self across the road with his arm around the semi-naked shoulders of a woman, not his wife. Neither does Plath, sitting in the car, notice this ghostly future self-staring at them, knowing their fate and helpless to warn them. No such anxiety or gloomy premonition clouded the actual day of the move. In a letter to her mother on 4 September, Plath described a fine, hot, sunny day for moving, although the house was shrouded in fog as she wrote. Now almost five months pregnant with her second child Nicholas, Plath appeared happy, if somewhat overwhelmed by the task ahead of her.

By Hughes's own admission in *Birthday Letters*, it was his dream to move to the deep country. His poem 'Error' is an affecting narrative of the accountability he felt for bringing Plath into his dreamland. He describes her as gallant, desperate and hopeful, her strangeness standing out as a point of curiosity in the small West Country town. Certainly Plath threw herself into town life, ironically much more than Hughes. But her letters from 1961 until she leaves Devon in late 1962, echo with a wistful longing for London and for what she calls a 'cultural' life. Yet this did not interfere with her determination to create a country home.

At the beginning of September 1961, Plath had many reasons to be excited. Not only did she have a new home and a second child on the way, but her brother Warren was due to arrive on 9 September for a six day visit. Writing home to his mother on the 10th, Warren described the reunion on North Tawton station, after which they drove to nearby Okehampton for eggs and mushrooms. The rest of the day was spent relaxing in the afternoon sun eating banana bread in Court Green's garden. During his stay, the Plaths and Hughes drove to Tintagel and ate a picnic on the sea cliffs, and went blackberrying near Hartland Point. Warren and Hughes worked on sanding an immense elm plank that would be placed in Plath's study to become her writing desk. The life of this elm plank is intriguing. In his poem 'The Table', Ted Hughes describes how the piece of wood was initially rough cut for coffin timber. Sanded by himself and Warren Plath, it lived in Plath's study where she used it to write some of her most memorable work. After her death, at some stage, Elizabeth Sigmund recalls it was moved downstairs into the big kitchen where meals were eaten. In the 1980s, Hughes sold it to Smith College, Northampton, Massachusetts, where it now hangs on a wall, complete with ink stains and pencil markings. Once more raging against readers of Plath, Hughes states in his poem that it is there to be stared at by the peanut-crunchers, no longer a desk, once more a board.

One of the first poems written on this desk was 'Wuthering Heights', potentially the first poem that Plath composed after her move to Devon.[5] It is interesting that she threw her imagination back up into the north of the country, taking inspiration from previous visits to Yorkshire. The poem went through many workings and re-workings, beginning life with a title of simply 'Withins' before becoming 'The Bald Truth About: Grass at Wuthering Heights', then 'The Grass', before settling upon 'Wuthering Heights'. It is a poem about the importance of place and the traces that can be left behind:

> Of people the air only
> Remembers a few odd syllables.
> It rehearses them moaningly:
> Black stone, black stone. (1990: 168)

There is certainly a sense of melancholy about this poem—a real feeling of openness and nothingness 'like being mailed into space' (1990: 167). Yet this is contrasted on 23 September with 'Blackberrying', a poem which Plath states is about the day spent with her brother Warren, blackberrying in the lanes near Hartland Point. This is a more comfortable poem, less disconcerting. Nevertheless, the ending again is about great space and nothingness and the din of the sea repeatedly smashing against the rocks. It is perhaps significant having moved from a tiny city flat to a large country house that Plath's first poems composed in Devon were preoccupied with space and wide, open skies.

The elm plank which Plath used as a writing desk. Now held at the Mortimer Rare Book Room, Smith College. (*Gail Crowther*)

By 27 September, Plath wrote to her mother that she was beginning to settle into some sort of routine in her new house. She worked in her study in a morning while Hughes minded Frieda and then they swopped for the afternoon. A local woman, Nancy Axworthy, who had cleaned the house for years agreed to work for Plath two days a week cleaning upstairs on a Tuesday and downstairs on a Thursday. Wanting to bring a little of New England to her garden in Devon, Plath planned to order some True Boston magnolia bushes and hoped that Santa would send some America corn seeds for the vegetable patch. Plath was pleased with her flower beds which were on the lawn just outside of the yellow front door beneath the living room and playroom windows. Elizabeth Sigmund recalls Plath planting some unusual grey rose bushes of which she was especially proud.

Two days later on the 29th, Plath wrote her final poems of the month—'Finisterre' and 'The Surgeon at 2 a.m.' Although composed on the same day, it is clear from the drafts that she started her ideas for 'Finisterre' first. Based on a location at the Pointe du Raz which Plath and Hughes had visited on their trip to France that summer, 'Finisterre' describes the rocky land's end overlooked by the statue of Our Lady of the Shipwrecked. With tales of battered shipwrecks in the nearby Baie des Trépassés (Bay of the Dead), the poem brings to life the flowers growing along the cliff edge, a kneeling peasant woman praying to the statue, and the small postcard stalls selling trinkets and crêpes. The Pointe du Raz is much changed today from the summer Plath walked the cliffs. The postcard stalls are replaced by a large, curved visitor's centre and shuttle buses run the short trip from the car park out to the headland. The dramatic cliffs and exploding sea do remain, however, as does the statue of Our Lady, still staring out across the ocean some fifty or more years later.

'The Surgeon at 2 a.m.' feels like a curious hybrid scene from *The Bell Jar* and imagery from an earlier poem that year, 'Tulips'. The clinical setting is a hospital in which the lumpen mass of a human body lies beneath the hands of a surgeon who squeaks and oozes his way through the insides:[6]

This is the lung-tree.
These orchids are splendid. They spot and coil like snakes.
The heart is a red-bell-bloom, in distress.
I am so small

Our Lady of the Shipwrecked statue at Pointe du Raz, Finisterre, France which features in Plath's poem 'Finisterre'. (*Gail Crowther*)

In comparison to these organs!
I worm and hack in a purple wilderness. (1990: 170–1)

Despite these feelings of smallness and inadequacy, by the end of the poem the narrating surgeon is quite certain of his power—he can remove limbs, perfect a body, create relics. The final lines show the charismatic pull of the surgeon for the patients, even in a drugged stupor:

I am the sun, in my white coat,
Gray faces, shuttered by drugs, follow me like flowers. (1990: 171)

'The Surgeon at 2 a.m.' is a fine example of a Plath poem that can be read intertextually. The atmosphere, tone, and imagery mix with other pieces of prose and poetry so clearly, it sometimes feels that all of Plath's work belongs on some large interlinked canvas. In light of poems written immediately before and after, the topic of this work seems an anomaly. However, placing it in the context of Plath's other work—completing final edits on *The Bell Jar*, sending out manuscripts of 'Tulips' to Jack Sweeney at the Woodberry Poetry Room at Harvard, and submitting poems such as 'Face Lift', 'A Life' and 'In Plaster' to various journals—the connected imagery is quite startling and worthy of a study in itself.

October saw Plath's personal and professional life shift somewhat. In a letter to her mother on 6 October, Plath said that she was now concentrating on her prose writing. Indeed, she had just that week finished her first women's magazine short story written in Devon. This is most likely to have been 'A Winter's Tale', the typescript of which is not held in any public archive. Plath playfully described how she and Hughes had been dreaming up plots as she was due to meet a fiction editor in London at the end of the month. Certainly the first half of October saw a concerted effort by Plath to get her stories published. On the 13th she submitted two more pieces of prose, 'Shadow Girl' and 'The Beggars' to A.M. Heath Agents. On the following day, 'Johnny Panic and the Bible of Dreams' was sent to *The Sewanee Review*. However, Plath was not neglecting her poetry, and on the 10 October she submitted to *The New Yorker* the first four poems she had written in her new home.[7] In her domestic life, Plath was further establishing a routine. Her sewing table was now set up in the bay window of the playroom, and she was planning to attend the local Anglican church at the end of the garden since she saw this as one of the best ways to 'grow' into the community. Plath also worked hard at keeping communication alive with friends and London based acquaintances. On 6 October she wrote to the poet Ruth Fainlight, sympathising about a threatened miscarriage and hoping to see her and her husband, the novelist Alan Sillitoe, during her London visit at the end of the month.[8]

Given Plath's later output, the middle of October was a quiet time. No poems, no letters, no prose. One reason for this can be found in a letter Plath wrote to her mother on the 22nd in which she described how tired she was beginning to feel by her pregnancy and her need to take naps in the afternoon. By 21 October, Plath and Heinemann had a contractual agreement to publish *The Bell Jar* which Heinemann noted was already delivered to them. Also on the 21st, Plath wrote her first poem of the month, 'Last Words', a beautiful muse on death and burial. This is also a poem about time, projecting and playing with haunting futurities of those who may at some stage find the narrator's buried, dead body. But not yet:

> Now they are nothing, they are not even babies.
> I imagine them without mother and fathers, like the first gods.
> They will wonder if I was important. (1990: 172)

'Last Words' is important as it was written the day before the poem which is often cited as the first hint of Plath's *Ariel* voice to come, 'The Moon and the Yew Tree'. Yet, one cannot help but think that 'Last Words' also hints at the change about to occur in Plath's poetic voice. There is an immediacy in the narrative style, a confrontational attitude towards death, a stunning assonance of word sounds and the characteristic blunt short sentences of later poems. Consider and read aloud the following lines:

> I do not trust the spirit. It escapes like steam
> In dreams through mouth-hole or eye-hole. I can't stop it.
> One day it won't come back. (1990: 172)

This theme of death and burial is picked up and expanded in the 'The Moon and the Yew Tree' written the following day. Al Alvarez recalls that this poem had its origins in sleeplessness.[9] One night in the early hours, as Plath was pacing the bedroom at Court Green, Hughes told her to look out of the window and write about what she could see. Their bedroom window looked across the front lawn to the row of headstones, St Peter's Church and the yew tree. However, this poem is much more than a poetical description of a night scene. It appears to be a psychological study ('The trees of the mind are black') set in a Gothic context ('Fumy, spirituous mists inhabit this place'). The narrator sees a disquieting moon which is 'terribly upset' and which shines with 'the O-gape of complete despair'. Certainly something mysterious has befallen the narrator. We do not discover what this might be, but she states a yearning and a sense of failure:

How I would like to believe in tenderness –
The face of the effigy, gentled by candles,
Bending, on me, in particular, its mild eyes.
I have fallen a long way. (1990: 173)

The yew tree in St Peter's Churchyard, North Tawton. This tree was visible from Plath's study and features in her poem 'The Moon and the Yew Tree'. (*Gail Crowther*)

The final message of the poem is bleak. The moon is blind to any sense of holiness and 'The message of the yew tree is blackness—blackness and silence' (1990: 173). Upon reading this poem, Ted Hughes claimed he was appalled and depressed. One can certainly see there is a darkness about this night time musing. But it is interesting to read this poem alongside letters Plath was writing at the time. The tone of most of her work contained a gentle melancholy. A letter written to her mother on the same day this poem was composed (the 22nd) repeated almost word for word some of the descriptions of the church. Plath was tired. She was missing London. She was trying to establish herself in a new town and a new home. She had by this stage attended her first church service and been left utterly disillusioned by the sermon which she described as 'awful'. The poem is not so shocking when read alongside other things she was writing and experiences she described.

The following day, the 23rd, Plath wrote 'Mirror', a much perkier description of reflections and doubles. Time once again is central to this poem, as is honesty and truth. The reflective surfaces of a mirror and a lake do not lie but reflect back exactly what they see. A woman may try to disguise this truth, turning to the moon or candles to soften the image, but ultimately it cannot be so. The reflective surface of the lake clearly states that there is no deterrent to the ravages of time:

> In me she has drowned a young girl, and in me an old woman
> Rises toward her day after day, like a terrible fish. (1990: 174)

In a letter finished to her mother on 30 October (but started four days earlier), Plath sounded excited about a London trip which was to take place the following day. She described how she would be collecting a prize for her poem 'Insomniac' and spending two days with friends Ruth Fainlight and Alan Sillitoe. On her second night in London, she was due to visit the theatre for the first time since leaving the city. Towards the end of the letter, however, Plath returned to serious subjects which were clearly playing on her mind—the high levels of Strontium-90 found in milk and the latest fallout shelter craze in America. This was a topic that in the months to come would help form a bond between the political consciences of Plath and Elizabeth Sigmund. In the meantime, Plath was glad to be hidden away in the country. In fact there was nowhere she would rather be. Amusingly, on the same day, Plath wrote to her friend Helga Huws, describing the 'ugly' town she had moved to and how homesick she felt for London. This conflicting presentation of the self is a key feature of Plath when her letters are viewed together. Often on the same day she would write, somewhat mischievously, opposing statements to different people. There is certainly a feeling that she wrote home what she believed her mother would *like* to hear, while letters to friends or to her brother contained a more 'honest' and open voice, somewhat sharper and wittier.

The final poem Plath wrote in October was on the 29th, two days before her trip to London. 'The Babysitters' is a lyrical collection of memories recalling a summer spent babysitting in Swampscott, Massachusetts with her close college friend Marcia Brown. The poem, set in 1951, begins quite wistfully: 'It is ten years now, since we rowed to Children's Island' and recounts a rare day off from work to visit a small, deserted island off the coast. In keeping with other poems of this period, one central thematic feature is the impact of time:

> A gallery of creaking porches and still interiors,
> Stopped and awful as a photograph of someone laughing,
> But ten years dead. (1990: 175)

In the final stanza, Plath plays around with time, the narrator suspending the day in some kind of preserved eternity of memory, while equally acknowledging the relentless passing of years:

> I see us floating there yet, inseparable—two cork dolls.
> What keyhole have we slipped through, what door has shut?
> The shadows of the grasses inched round like the hands of a clock,
> And from our opposite continents we wave and call.
> Everything has happened. (1990: 175)

As October came to a close, Plath celebrated her twenty-ninth birthday and saw one ambition fulfilled—the publication of a short story in a women's magazine. On 28 October, 'The Perfect Place' featured in *My Weekly*; a love story set in the vicinity of Whitby, Yorkshire, featuring a Canadian heroine, Joanna, and her unsatisfactory fiancé, Kenneth. Luckily, as is often the way in such stories, Joanna is saved from a life with the controlling, boring Kenneth by Simon, the dashing and artistic son of her boarding house landlady. In a somewhat surreal ending, Joanna finds herself sitting in a Whitby pub at night time, in the shadow of the ruined Abbey, talking to a parrot.

November was a quiet month for Plath. On the 5th she wrote to her mother how she was dreading the onslaught of winter, but looking forward to another trip to London later that month. She had once again been to a Sunday service in St Peter's Church:

> Went to the Anglican chapel evensong again tonight. It's a peaceful little well on Sunday evenings, and I do love the organ, the bell-ringing and the hymn singing, and muse on the stained-glass windows during the awful sermons. (1988: 435)

The following day brought much happier news. Plath received notification that she had won a Fellowship from The Eugene F. Saxton Memorial Trust worth $2,000, to be paid quarterly. This grant was to support prose writing over the coming year. At some stage between 6–14 November, Plath developed an ingenious idea. Since her first novel, *The Bell Jar*, had already been accepted by Heinemann, she wrote to her editor James Michie asking him to delay publication of the novel. This way, she could submit quarterly sections of the book to the Saxton Memorial Trust and this would remove the pressure for her to *have* to write something over the coming twelve months. Heinemann were happy to accommodate. In fact their greater concern seemed to be whether Plath was certain *The Bell Jar* would not incite any libel action from characters represented in the story. In papers contained at Smith College, Plath outlined her reasons why she felt this was unlikely, demonstrating ways in which she had fictionalised certain places, events, and people. Nevertheless, reading her justifications in this way only serves to highlight how flimsy some of the disguises actually are and perhaps further explains why Plath kept this novel on the low-down with family and friends and published under the pseudonym Victoria Lucas.

Within days of receiving the letter from the Saxton Trust, Plath wrote informing her mother of the good news and providing further details of town and domestic life. She described witnessing a hunt meeting in the town square which she found oddly impressive, despite her sympathy for the fox. Further furniture had been purchased for Court Green, in particular for her study. She was now the proud owner of a comfortable chair upholstered in black corduroy with a high, scrolled back as well as a 'nice, wood' chair for typing. One feels in these letters throughout 1961 and 1962 that Plath is delighting in nest building for the first time, establishing a home and a working space that pleases her aesthetic eye. Colours and textures appear important and are ultimately themes that will bleed from her domestic life into her poetic imagery. On the 20th, Plath wrote to her mother that she was planning a trip to London 'this week' to order carpets. Despite looking in Exeter and Plymouth, she could not find any to suit her taste—turkey-red for her study and staircase and green for Frieda's room. Presumably in response to a worried comment regarding the Saxton grant, Plath assured her mother she had already written 'stuff' which could be submitted over the coming year, so there was no pressure on her to write at all. Gleefully, Plath informed her mother how much money there was to be made from her and Hughes's draft manuscripts (which she called 'scrap paper') stating that she had just sold 130 pages to Indiana University for £100. Little could she know how these pieces of 'scrap paper' would in future years become invaluable to scholars keen to explore the poetic construction of a Plath poem.

Professionally, despite writing no poems this month, Plath was still working on other projects. As well as completing the typescript of *The Bell Jar*, she was also finalising the editing of a small pamphlet of poems called *American Poetry Now* for *The Critical Quarterly*. On 8 November she wrote to Howard Moss of *The New Yorker* discussing the publication of her own poem 'Blackberrying', offering one or two changes. The 10th November saw her review of a children's book, *General Jodpur's Conversion,* appear in *The New Statesman*. This would be the start of a new strand of Plath's career as contemporary critic and reviewer. Between then and her death in February 1963, she would review many books both in print and on the radio, and was invited to become a regular panel member on the new BBC programme *The Critics* which sadly began in May 1963, just months after her death.

The following month, on the 7th, Plath wrote to her mother how depressed she felt about a range of political issues—in particular an article in *The Nation* by Fred J. Cook called 'Juggernaut: The Warfare State', and the ensuing shelter craze erupting in America. In fact she was so worried that she was not sleeping at night. Her allegiance lay firmly with the nuclear disarmers.

> Thank goodness there is none of this idiotic shelter business in England. I just wish England had the sense to be neutral, for it is quite obvious she would be "obliterated" in any nuclear war, and for this reason I am very much behind the nuclear disarmers here. (1988: 438)

This was a topic of concern that Plath was to share with Elizabeth Sigmund, as they discovered during their first meeting. Sigmund recalls Plath's horror when she told her about a local man who had visited his doctor requesting suicide pills to take in the event of a nuclear attack. Sadly for Plath, the CND meetings in Devon only began after her death, and although Sigmund herself became involved she found it difficult to dedicate time and energy to the movement while raising her children. It seems likely that Plath too would have experienced this challenge had she lived long enough to become involved. Nevertheless, Sigmund recalls Plath speaking often about her concerns regarding the nuclear arms race and recounts the occasion when she had taken Frieda to watch the end of the Aldermaston March in Trafalgar Square, London in 1960. Plath's tensions and worries are understandable in this historical context. She wrote to her mother how it sometimes felt crazy to raise a family in a world gone so mad; and these fears of war, annihilation, deformed children and the threat of nuclear holocaust inform the mood of later poems such as 'Fever 103', 'Getting There', 'Thalidomide', 'Mary's Song' and 'Brasilia'.

Perhaps somewhat paralysed and exhausted from these anxieties and her pregnancy, Plath did little professionally all month. In the 7 December letter to her mother, she admitted feeling lazy and was writing 'terribly little', but had ordered carpets for the house during her London trip. Conversely, in a letter to the poet Thom Gunn written the day before, Ted Hughes was thankful that London now felt further off than America or the Continent to him and how freeing this was. The city, he believed, jammed up his work and writing with its 'smog of static'. Although December was another month in which Plath wrote no poetry, she did see some of her recent work accepted by major publications. On 12 December she wrote to Brian Cox of *The Critical Quarterly* to say how delighted she was with the pamphlet *American Poetry Now*, which she had finished editing the previous month. On the same day, Plath received notification from Howard Moss that *The New Yorker* wanted to extend its First Reading Contract to her.[10] Six days later, Plath replied to Moss extending her thanks for the contract and discussing the up and coming publication of 'The Moon and the Yew Tree' and 'Mirror'. There had been some discussion about the title of the latter poem, originally called 'Mirror Talk'. Moss was concerned with the word 'talk' in the title, stating that *everyone* was using it since the song 'Happy Talk', from the musical *South Pacific*, became a hit. Plath, was happy to oblige and make changes, removing the offending word and stating modestly that with a few exceptions she regarded herself as rather 'numb' at titles.

The rest of the month saw Plath making preparations for Christmas in her new home. A card written to her mother and brother on the 15th shows that she and Hughes had been exploring Dartmoor and finding good picnic sites for when Aurelia Plath was due to visit the following summer. Further home improvements had been taking place with the arrival of an off-white and rose Indian rug for their bedroom, along with a goatskin rug for the floor at the foot of the bed. This latter rug apparently delighted Frieda, who loved to roll on it. Plath was expecting delivery of a small evergreen tree which she planned to decorate with home-made German spice cookies in tin foil and baubles and birds from Woolworths. She felt it important to keep all of the Plath traditions alive. There is something melancholy about this letter. Perhaps it is the merest hint of homesickness or her humorous comments regarding town locals who she did not yet know but hoped to slowly become friendly with:

> The town itself is fascinating—a solid body of inter-related locals (very curious), then all these odd peripheral people—Londoners, ex-Cockneys, Irish. I look forward to getting to know them slowly. (1988: 439)

Plath and Hughes had been unable to send presents for Christmas due to the expense of moving, and they hoped that the family would understand. Three days later on the 18th, she again wrote to Aurelia and Warren Plath, sending them some colour photographs of Frieda standing outside of Court Green, pointing out the gnarled branch of an ancient honeysuckle growing to the right of the front door. Earlier that day she had driven into Exeter for some final Christmas shopping and described the white frost which made the cows and sheep look pink.

Renovations in Court Green continued with electricians fitting power plugs in four rooms so electric heaters could be moved around, and Plath finally got hold of some red corduroy to make living room curtains and a window seat cover. Hughes had finished the last of the floor painting and was about to begin making a doll's crib for Frieda's Christmas present. This crib survives today, another relic stored in Smith College, again in remarkable condition. It is a small, rocking cradle which Plath painted white and decorated with bluebirds, hearts and flowers. The coloured paint is so vibrant that it still looks shiny and wet. The front headboard of the crib is adorned with green ivy, blue flowers and a red heart; the back with a blue four-leafed clover and more red hearts. There is something a little ghostly about such realia preserving their solidity through time. Although removed from their original context, they do retain their power. Perhaps in some ways this is the importance of material culture; objects *do* have the ability to engage our imagination, our fantasies. It seems unlikely that Hughes, as he cut and planed the wood, or Plath as she painted the completed cradle, could ever have known or thought that this object would be preserved for history in a college archive. Yet there it remains, an uncanny relic of a family Christmas. Curiously, towards the end of her life, Plath stated that she loved 'the thinginess of things' and in a sense objects can cross boundaries to mediate between the past and present, the living and the dead.

On 29 December, sitting in front of a crackling wood fire, Plath wrote to her mother that she had spent the happiest and fullest Christmas. The carpets had arrived in time for the holiday, making Court Green the perfect Christmas house. Neighbours had delivered presents and flowers and Plath looked forward to establishing future Christmases in her own home. In a second letter written on the same day, congratulations were sent to Warren Plath celebrating his recent engagement to Margaret Wetzel, with Plath already asking when the wedding would be and what she might buy for a present.

Frieda's crib built by Ted Hughes and decorated with birds and flowers by Sylvia Plath. Now held in the Mortimer Rare Book Room, Smith College. (*Gail Crowther*)

Although Plath wrote no poems or prose this month, on 28 December she sent out three batches of work to various journals: eight poems to *Harper's*, four to *The Observer*, and a copy of her story 'Johnny Panic and the Bible of Dreams' to *The Chelsea Review*. Only four poems from this submission set would eventually be accepted the following year—'Private Ground' and 'Leaving Early' by *Harper's* and 'The Rival' and 'Finisterre' by *The Observer*. Once again, Plath's attempt to publish 'Johnny Panic' had failed; this story would never be published in her lifetime.

The end of 1961 and the start of 1962 were celebrated at a Saturday night party on 30 December at George and Marjorie Tyrer's flat in the town square at North Tawton. George Tyrer was the bank manager of National Provincial Bank, and Marjory was his Irish wife. Their fifteen-year-old daughter, Nicola, who would become a regular visitor to Court Green in the coming months, remembers Plath and Hughes as standing out at the party like exotic birds. Plath, heavily pregnant and resplendent in a blue Chinese jacket, sipped sherry and finally met some of the local people she had previously expressed a wish to get to know. Over the coming five months, Plath's X-ray vision would take in every detail of the Tyrer's home, furniture, dress, and family stories and record them in her Journal notes. The Tyrers were not the only locals caught under Plath's detailed surveillance. Next to Court Green were Rose and Percy Key. In the cottage next to the Keys were Mr and Mrs Watkins. Across the street, the formidable Mrs Hamilton. A mixture of North Tawton locals and ex-Londoners, Plath appeared fascinated by their lives. Updated on a regular basis, her notes describe minute details from the lives of her neighbours: the wallpaper in their homes, the colour of rugs, the smell of cooking, types of cakes eaten at tea, their histories and patterns of speech. Simultaneously, she casts an amused eye over her own interaction with them, describing her reliance on conversational clichés and noting tart observations about their behaviour and motivations. This neighbourly surveillance runs from March to June and is some of Plath's richest, wittiest journal writing. It also gives us a flavour of presumably how her (now 'missing') 1962 Journal would read—that immediate and sharp *Ariel* voice beginning to break through even in her personal prose.

From January 1962 onwards, despite Plath's 'missing' Journals, we do have an additional resource in her Letts wall calendar. On this, Plath recorded the minutiae of her everyday life. The idea was to list every task or job that needed completing in order to feel a sense of achievement at the end of the day. As such, Plath's calendar informs us what she was cooking, eating, who was visiting, when she wrote letters, when she placed grocery orders and which days she washed her hair. This wall calendar provides a fascinating text into the canvas of Plath's work and further allows an intertextual reading of the domestic and the professional. Often the two blur into each other in astonishing ways, which further informs us how Plath received inspiration, how she manipulated her poetical imagination from personal events into universal significance. Furthermore, the trivia of everyday life is not without its interest. Henry Miller claimed that the writing of certain authors for him was so charged that he could become excited by reading an expenses account! (Wilson, 1999).

For the first two weeks of January, Plath did very little. She baked sand tarts, apple pies, and lemon cake pudding. She wrote Christmas thank-you notes and awaited the arrival of her second child, due on the 11th. In a letter to her mother dated 12 January, Plath wrote that she was feeling lazy and relying on sleeping pills to allow her ten hours sleep each night. She had not worked in her study for three weeks because she felt 'too ponderous' and she was struggling with prickly and bloated arms. All of her rugs had now arrived, which further cheered her and helped make the rooms feel warmer, but all of her energy was spent on waiting to give birth

Nicholas Farrar Hughes was born at 11.55 p.m. on 17 January in the guest room at Court Green, delivered by the local midwife, Winifred Davies, and in the presence of Ted Hughes. Plath described in both a letter to her mother and her surviving journal notes of Nicholas's dramatic arrival. How the baby, seemingly struggling, finally and suddenly gushed out onto the bed in a wave of water. Plath's notes on the birth of Nicholas are honest and moving. Hughes, worried about the effect of her words, withheld them from publication for many years. Presumably this was because initially Plath was surprised at giving birth to a boy and not sure that she liked him. But very quickly she got used the idea and from that point onwards adored him and his dark smiley-ness. In fact, some of Plath's most tender and beautiful poems are written to Nicholas, such as 'By Candlelight', 'Nick and the Candlestick', and 'The Night Dances'. In order to allow Hughes a good night's sleep to deal with Frieda and running the house, Plath and Nicholas slept in the guest bedroom overlooking the courtyard and the elms.

When Plath began writing to her mother seven days later on 24 January, she had just spent her first whole day out of bed and finally felt as though things were calming down.

> This morning I took a hot bath first thing, put on proper clothes and feel very fresh. I simply wore through the seams of all the underwear and maternity skirts and tights I wore in the last months and looked like a great, patchy monster at the end. (1988: 444)

Neighbours had all been kind, bringing gifts and food but the letter was interrupted and only finished on the 27th as Plath came down with milk fever and a temperature of 103 degrees. Journal notes describe a culture clash between her expectations of the medical treatment she felt she should receive and how the local doctor, Hugh Webb, viewed the situation. He was not happy that Plath had taken her own temperature or that she demanded medicine to help bring her fever down. Insomuch as Plath worked hard to fit into town life, she was not prepared to be submissive over matters that were important to her. Interestingly, as one of her neighbours Percy Key got sick over the coming months, Plath marvelled at the lack of interest and knowledge that he and his wife displayed regarding his diagnosis and treatment. It seemed incredible to her that they asked so few questions; their vagueness is reproduced in a poem written about Percy Key called 'Among the Narcissi' in which he is described as recuperating from 'something on the lung.'

By 31 January, Plath wrote to her mother that she felt fully recovered from the milk fever, but was taking long afternoon naps to rest. The previous night had been her first without sleeping pills and her hope was to continue without them. But she was feeling homesick:

> I have got awfully homesick for you since the last baby—and for the Cape
> and deep snow and such things. Can't wait for your visit. (1988: 445)

She and Hughes had decided to buy a new radio and thus followed a light-hearted account of life in the country. *They* thought they would need to go to London to buy a good radio but were assured that North Tawton had *the* best electricians. Sure enough, they now owned a radio cabinet made of matt-finished walnut with an aerial fixed onto the roof. The previous evening they had enjoyed listening to a production of *Agamemnon* by Aeschylus. Given that Plath and Hughes were both rising stars on the BBC, they were keen to have a decent machine on which they could listen to their own broadcasts too. In a letter written on the same day to her Aunt Dot (Dorothy Benotti), Plath reiterated her homesickness for snow and family reunions and how difficult it was to heat Court Green in the depths of a Devonshire winter.

One poem exists from January 1962, 'New Year on Dartmoor', though it is not accurately dated. Given that on the 12th Plath had not worked in her study for three weeks, it is most likely to date from towards the end of the month, after the birth of Nicholas and her recovery from milk fever. Typed on the verso of early drafts of *The Bell Jar*, this nine line poem begins with the title 'The Bald Truth About: Frost on Dartmoor in the New Year' and appears to be about a child's bewilderment at the peculiar, slippery frost. It is perhaps not one of Plath's best poems and yet there is a tenderness about the narrator observing her child who has no language skills to describe the scene. The characters in the poem are curiously detached, not part of the landscape at all, but rather observers: 'We have only come to look,' they say (1990: 176).

Plath's Letts calendar shows that for all of January she kept shifting and delaying writing her first quarterly progress report for the Saxton Trust. Despite appearing as a designated task on the first page of January, Plath does not actually complete and mail this until the following month on 10 February. Usually organised and rarely shifting work in this way, her calendar reveals that Plath was perhaps struggling to cope in a cold house with a dependent newborn, a domestic routine, and her own writing. In fact the only other occasion in which we can see Plath shifting and delaying work in this manner is during the weeks before her death.

From 1 February, Plath appeared to be back into some sort of routine, although throughout this whole month she would write no poems at all. She was cooking banana bread and stew and entertaining neighbours, such as Marjorie Tyrer and her immediate neighbour, Rose Key. In a letter written on the first day of the month to a Mrs Eaton who had made blankets and pot holders which Plath received for Christmas, she described the weather in Devon as grim, but that she had discovered the first snowdrops and primroses in the garden. On 6 February, Plath took Nicholas to visit another neighbour, Mrs Hamilton, who lived across the road from Court Green in a white cottage called Crispens. Mrs Hamilton it later transpired was through some complicated lineage related to the midwife Winifred Davies, and subsequently Elizabeth Sigmund also discovered that she was related to Davies on the maternal side of her family. The following day Plath wrote to her mother how behind she was with everything domestic. Nicholas had already settled into a feeding routine, waking her at 2 a.m. and 6 a.m. each day, and so she hoped by the end of the month to be back in her study working and writing. This is a reflective letter, however. Plath was missing family, she was missing her closest friends and she was missing American snow. She likened the six months of English damp, rain and blackness as being like the six months Persephone had to spend with Pluto in the underworld. A week later, Plath was still struggling to rise above the domestic drudge and shake off her exhaustion. In a letter to her mother on 13 February, she said she was sleeping all of the time and when not sleeping the days were a whirl of baths, laundry, meals, and feeding. However, there was a glimmer of hope. 'Nicholas is absolutely darling' (1988: 447) writes Plath. Furthermore, she had discovered some double-headed snowdrops in the garden along with the first daffodil shoots.

The rest of the month appeared to be spent entertaining neighbours, and on the 18th she hosted a lunch for the writer Charles Causley who lived relatively nearby in Launceston. It is interesting to see from the surviving journal notes of this time, the differing expectations Plath had regarding her involvement with North Tawton locals. Perhaps touched by the kindness of her neighbours following the birth of Nicholas, Plath returned their kindness by visiting her immediate neighbour, Rose Key, while her husband Percy was in hospital, and calling on the Tyrers in their flat above the bank having heard that George had suffered a mild heart attack. Yet, when unexpected callers dropped into Court Green, such as Mrs Hamilton and Nicola Tyrer, Plath's irritation and outrage are barely concealed. Certainly the journal account of Mrs Hamilton 'invading' Plath's study while she is working gives a clear message of how essential and valuable Plath regarded her writing time. This is hardly surprising given that Plath's poetic output had all but stopped for four months. Whether at this stage Plath fully realised the necessity of her writing time is unknown. It is not until two months later that she states in a letter it is only through having good quality writing time that she can bear being a wife, mother, and completing domestic chores as well. Perhaps more telling about this incident is Plath's admission that her anger was not with Mrs Hamilton for her uninvited visit, but rather Ted Hughes for being ineffectual at stopping the invasion of her study: 'My anger at Ted being a man, not at Mrs H., really' (2000: 651).

Towards the end of February Plath appeared to start recovering from her winter depression. She wrote to her mother on the 24th that she was feeling in fine shape and that the first daffodils had bloomed. Her son continued to delight her:

> He smiled at me a few times this week and is so sweet—a little sweet-smelling peach. I feel I really *enjoy* him.... (1988: 447)

Beginning to use her brain again, she was undertaking BBC Third Programme courses in French and German. The cold weather ground on though, and Court Green was so cold that she and Hughes were sleeping in the babies' bedroom, which was the warmest room in the house.

At the beginning of March, Plath experienced her first snow at Court Green, pretty and exquisite looking but lasting only a matter of hours. On 4 March, she was managing two and half hours each morning in her study and hoped to increase this to four hours per day when she could face rising at 6 a.m. She informed her mother that she was working on something that may 'turn into' a novel:

> I am beginning work on something amusing which I hope turns into a book (novel), but may just be happy piddling. I find long things much easier on my nature than poems—not so intensely demanding or depressing if not brought off. (1988: 448)

There are a couple of possibilities as to what this work may have been. The first is that it was her early ideas for *Three Women*, although given that this long poem for three voices was a piece commissioned by the BBC as a radio play, it seems unlikely Plath would be treating it in a novelistic manner at its inception. The second possibility is that she had started work on the mysterious 'second' novel, which according to Aurelia Plath, picked up the narrative where *The Bell Jar* left off—detailing Esther Greenwood's move to England, marriage, and babies. This manuscript, claims Aurelia Plath, was intended as a birthday present for Ted Hughes, but Plath destroyed the only copy in a bonfire during the summer of 1962 after discovering his infidelity. There is no evidence of this novel beyond Aurelia Plath's testimony—no working notes and no other reference to it in letters. Since Plath's journals are 'missing' from this period of her life, we simply cannot know whether she discussed it within those pages. The third possibility is that Plath had already begun work on the novel which we know she partially completed (now also 'missing' along with her journals), initially titled *The Interminable Loaf*, then *Doubletake* and finally *Double Exposure*. This seems the most unlikely possibility. Given the plot of this novel deals with an idyllic marriage gone wrong, it seems much more likely that work on this started later in the summer. Indeed Plath's Letts calendar shows a note reminding herself to begin writing it in August of that year.

At some stage during March, Plath did begin work on *Three Women* and completed it by the end of the month. This poem for three voices deals with childbirth and loss in all of its many guises, set within 'a maternity ward and roundabout'. The first voice is a wife giving birth to a son; the second voice is a secretary suffering a miscarriage; and the third voice a young student who gives her baby away for adoption. In a letter written a few months later, Plath informed her mother that this radio play had been accepted by the BBC. It was inspired, she wrote, by an Ingmar Bergman film called *So Close to Life* (1958). Plath likely saw this film the first time it aired in England sometime between 24 February and 29 March 1961, at the Academy Cinema in Oxford Street (now demolished). Indeed a review of this film appears in *The Times* on page eight, the same day her collection of poems *The Colossus* was reviewed on page fifteen. The film, set in a maternity ward, deals with three women: Stina (Eva Dahlbeck), a happy, healthy wife who gives birth to a son; Cecilia (Ingrid Thulin), a secretary, who suffers from a miscarriage; and Hjördiss (Bibi Andersson), an unmarried, teenage tearaway who contemplates an abortion. Bergman successfully wrong-foots the audience by ending the film with the death of Stina's baby and the decision by Hjördiss to keep her baby. The context in which Plath saw this film was powerful. Within weeks of her own appendectomy and miscarriage, the experience of the three women in a clinical setting must have struck a particularly poignant chord. Certainly, as with her experiences in France, Plath stored this in her imagination for over a year before it found expression in her only radio play.

As well as returning to her writing, Plath spent the first half of March further visiting her neighbours, a Mr and Mrs Watkins in Court Green Cottages and again the Tyrers. Her wry eye was once again cast over their house furnishings, friends, and family. On the 12th, Plath wrote to her mother that she was feeling sentimental and thinking about passing on her china and Grammy's desk to Frieda:

> One feels a girl is the one to appreciate the domestic things, for she is the one who uses them. I know I shall reserve my treasures for Frieda. I am getting very sentimental about family things. (1988: 449)

Despite what she referred to as the 'insane' sermons, she was arranging a baptism for Frieda and Nicholas at St Peter's Church in the town. These letters, as with earlier ones, have a hint of homesickness. Throughout 1961–62, Plath repeatedly stated how she would like someone 'from home' to admire her babies and her house. Perhaps this sense of isolation was felt more keenly in the deep country than when Plath was living a busier life in London and seeing more people. Certainly there is a sense that she wants to see her friends. On this same day she wrote to her friend Clarissa Roche, inviting her to come and stay, and then an undated letter from March to another London based friend, Ruth Fainlight, begs her to visit, stating how 'mad' Plath is for someone to talk to. The women in North Tawton, claimed Plath, were like a 'cattery'.

Despite her seeming loneliness for familiar faces, Plath was enjoying being back in her study working again. To Clarissa Roche, she claimed she was nearly done with a 'grossly amateur' novel (presumably *The Bell Jar*) and towards the end of the month she received word from *Harper's* that they had accepted two poems for publication: 'Leaving Early' and 'Private Ground'. In other professional areas, Plath had been invited by Marvin Kane of the BBC to take part in a new programme called *What Made You Stay?* in which Americans living in England were asked to explain their decision to settle in the country. Plath was keen to take part and invited Marvin Kane to Court Green with a portable tape recorder to carry out the interview. In her letter to him, dated 23 March, she wrote how she missed London so much more than Hughes but how it was impossible for her to visit there right now, even for a day, with the baby so dependent on her.

On Sunday 25 March, Frieda Rebecca Hughes and Nicholas Farrar Hughes were baptised in St Peter's Church by the Reverend Lane. Nicholas wore a christening gown of Limerick lace made from a wedding dress belonging to Marjorie Tyrer's grandmother and was accompanied into church by Plath's neighbour, Rose Key. Marjorie Tyrer had planned to carry out this duty but was ill with bronchitis and unable to attend. Frieda wore a blue French coat and pinafore, and according to Plath, both behaved beautifully in church. The weather was still grim and Plath claimed to be suffering from what she termed the 'March megrims', but they had been treated to one sunny day when she stayed outside from sunrise to sunset working in the garden. In fact, she refers to herself as a devout gardener despite not really knowing much about it. This love of planting and tending and growing is one aspect of Plath which has been overlooked in her biographies. The delight she experienced from working her flower beds and vegetable patch and trimming the grass is a recurring theme throughout 1962 and something that she continued to maintain single-handedly once she was living in Court Green alone (no small feat given there were acres of land).

April brought better weather and a burst of creativity. Plath wrote six poems, completed work for the BBC, and engaged in more socialising with neighbours. On the 1st of the month, celebrating Frieda's second birthday, Plath wrote to R. B. Silvers at *Harper's* expressing her pleasure at their acceptance of her two poems, 'Leaving Early' and 'Private Ground'. The following week saw Plath day after day writing new poems. On the 2nd, 'Little Fugue', on the 4th, 'An Appearance' and 'Crossing the Water', on the 5th, 'Among the Narcissi', and on the 7th, 'Pheasant'. These poems seemed to derive from a diverse range of inspirations. 'Little Fugue' is a muse on the remembrance of a dead father; 'An Appearance' is about the unrelenting work of an organised housewife (initially this poem was titled 'The Methodical Woman'); and 'Crossing the Water' is a reflection on sailing across Rock Lake at night in Canada. Further poems written in April take their inspiration from Plath's immediate surroundings in Court Green. One must, of course, be careful in terms of reading the poems as transparently autobiographical. However, by Plath's own admission in a 1962 interview with Peter Orr for the British Council, she did write about things and emotions immediately relevant to her, which she then transformed into something creative. 'Among the Narcissi' is about her sick neighbour, Percy Key, walking on the hill in Court Green's garden among the small white-yellow flowers. This subject is confirmed in a later letter to her mother. 'Pheasant' is about the appearance of a bird among the elms on the hill and in the snow-covered, cobbled courtyard. Addressed to 'you', the narrator makes a plea to the unseen person not to kill the bird but allow it to wander among the narcissi and settle in the elm. In fact the pheasant appears so settled, it is the narrator who is transposed into a sense of unbelonging:

It was sunning in the narcissi.

I trespass stupidly. Let be, let be. (1990: 191)

On 5 April, Plath also submitted several poems for publication—four to *The New Yorker* and eight to the BBC. On the 7th she made further arrangements to collect Marvin Kane from North Tawton railway station to record her BBC interview for *What Made You Stay?* Plath's letter confirming his visit is witty and sharp. Look out, she tells him, for someone covered in straw and red mud at the railway station—it will be her. And she warns him that the gale force winds have carried off all of her lettuces and deposited large spiders everywhere, mostly in her coffee cup before breakfast. She had booked Kane into the local inn, The Burton Arms, which because it had 'squeaked' into the Automobile Association (AA) book, she felt sure would not be too fearsome.

In a letter to her mother the following day, Plath bemoaned the three weeks of terrible weather and the disruption of having the downstairs floors concreted. Learning they would take two weeks to dry before she could lay linoleum left her even more fed up. To cheer herself up she had been:

...painting odd bits of grubby wood furniture—a table, chair—white with designs, very primitive, of hearts and flowers, which cheers me up and should look gay in the playroom. (1988: 451)

The furniture survives in Smith College archives, remarkably intact—a long white trestle table with a large heart painted in the centre and on each corner, an upright chair with hearts and flowers on the back, and a wastepaper basket with a large heart-shaped apple on the side. Elizabeth Sigmund remembers these items vividly from the playroom where she took afternoon tea that spring. Seeing this furniture preserved in an archive is slightly eerie, as though the past has suddenly crept unexpectedly into the present, evoking the dead, evoking the 'thinginess of things'.

Furniture painted by Sylvia Plath from the playroom in Court Green. Now held in the Mortimer Rare Book Room, Smith College. (*Karen V. Kukil, Mortimer Rare Book Room, Smith College*)

In this same letter, Plath also related other bits of news to her mother. George Tyrer the bank manager was being retired due to ill-health and Plath wrote how sorry she felt to be losing the company of his wife Marjorie and how much she liked their teenage daughter Nicola (Plath's journal notes claim the exact opposite). She informed her mother that *The Colossus* would be published in America by Knopf on the 14th May and that she was pleased with the edition. Over the previous two weeks she had picked 300 daffodils and jonquils from the garden but still she longed for some sunny weather.

On 10 April, Marvin Kane arrived to interview Plath bringing with him his wife, Kathy and an acquaintance with her two young daughters. The recorded interview took place in the sitting room at Court Green with Plath providing confident and humorous reasons why she chose to stay in England. Indeed some of her answers are so funny, you can clearly hear Marvin Kane stifling his laughter in the background. However, Plath's account to her mother of the Kane's visit is less cheerful:

[The Kanes]...brought an acquaintance with two of the most ghastly children I have ever seen—two girls of five and six. They had no inner life, no notion of obedience, and descended shrieking on Frieda's toys, running up and down through the house with muddy boots.... (1988: 452)

Luckily, she had recovered enough two days later to begin an extensive and complex poem 'Elm', a piece which would keep her busy for a full week, working and re-working ideas and imagery. Beginning with two differing titles 'Wind in the Great Elm' and 'The Sea at the Door', this sprawling poem covers twenty-two draft pages as Plath manipulates and transforms her original ideas into the poem we now know as 'Elm'. Initially this is an uneasy collection of imagery; the elm on the ancient hill eats the moon and the wind. The noise of her branches disturbs the narrator's sleep, terrifies children. But gradually the tone changes into something more complex: loss, the yearning for love, an agitated heart. Some of the imagery from the early drafts of 'Elm' reappears months later in the poem 'Words', suggesting that Plath retained and re-worked drafts. This furthermore supports the notion that Plath's work really can be read intertextually, like one long poem with interlinking themes and ideas. The following month, Plath would read and dedicate 'Elm' to her friend Ruth Fainlight who was visiting Court Green with her husband, Alan Sillitoe.

On 16 April, as Plath continued to grapple with 'Elm', she also found time to write letters to her sculptor friend, Leonard Baskin, and to her mother. The letter to Baskin takes a conciliatory tone apologising for an unpleasant visit that occurred while Plath and Hughes were still living at Chalcot Square in London during April 1961. Having given birth to Frieda just a year earlier, tired and with little space, Plath had struggled with Baskin sleeping on the sofa in the living room, tiptoeing around the flat while he slept until midday and having to cook meals which he seemingly often didn't eat. In fact, this letter by Plath is quite revealing. She openly states that writing is her life blood and it is only *that* which allows her to be domestic and motherly, for she cannot sustain the latter without the consolations of the former. She begs Baskin to come and visit in Devon so that they can erase the sour memories of their last meeting which continued to grieve both her and Hughes. In *Bitter Fame*, Dido Merwin offers the opinion that Plath never apologised and never saw the error of her ways. However, this letter is proof that clearly this was not the case and Plath even goes as far as to describe her 'fearsome nature' to Baskin. On the same day, in a cheerful letter to her mother, Plath wrote how she never knew it was possible to get so much joy out of babies ('I do think mine are special' p. 452). She loved Court Green and was picking 600 daffodils each week and still they showed no sign of diminishing. The hardest part for Plath was having no relatives of her own to admire her babies and her garden. Because of Plath's determination to stay in England from 1960 onwards, even after the breakdown of her marriage, her yearning for home and family is often unacknowledged, yet what her unpublished letters reveal is a very genuine wistfulness for New England and for the people that she loved.

Although Elizabeth Sigmund remembers her first meeting with Plath taking place around February/March time of this year, the first time Plath recorded a meeting was on 17 April when Elizabeth and her husband David Compton were invited to Court Green for tea. Elizabeth records her memories of this meeting in the opening section of this book, but it is significant to note Plath's delight at finding a friend who shared her political concerns. A 'committed woman' as Plath expressed it. Over the years it has been claimed that the friendship between Plath and Sigmund was short-lived and consisted of nothing more than a few meetings. However, even the most cursory glance at Plath's 1962 calendar shows this to be inaccurate. Furthermore, this does not take into account the letters and phone calls which also took place. Of equal significance is the fact that it was Elizabeth Sigmund who Plath turned to when she realised her marriage was under threat, driving to stay with her upon the discovery of Hughes's infidelity.

Later in the day following Elizabeth's visit, a more sombre affair took place, with the collapse of Plath's neighbour, Percy Key. Over the next two months, Plath would document his demise in her journal notes, culminating in the fine, epic poem 'Berck-Plage' written the day after Percy's funeral at the end of June.

The rest of April was taken up with neighbourly visits, farewell teas and dinners with the Tyrers and a visit from Hughes's Aunt Hilda and cousin Vicky. A Swedish photographer, Siv Arb, also arrived to take some photographs of Ted Hughes, but with friends and family staying, Plath was keen to make sure Arb made the last train back to London on the same day that she arrived. Having finished 'Elm' on the 19th, Plath's writing ceased once again as she dealt with domestic matters and hosting visitors. By the 25th, in a birthday card to her mother, Plath wrote how immensely happy she was in North Tawton and that her garden in Court Green was like a fairy tale, even more beautiful than the Cambridge Backs. The daffodils were in full bloom and Plath could not help but admire her favourite section of flowers which were strewn on the hill at the back of the garden beneath the apple trees. Finally she had spring fever!

The following day, on the 26th, George MacBeth of the BBC wrote to Plath that he would like to hold onto three of her poems for a future broadcast of *The Poet's Voice*. The poems were all fairly new and written since her move to Court Green—'Blackberrying', 'The Surgeon at 2 a.m.', and 'The Babysitters'. In a letter four days later to Marvin Kane, Plath wrote she hoped that he would be able to make something of her interview for the BBC. She gleefully described how much fun she had had, but lamented that she was not a more interesting subject. Her letter to Kane continues relating her gardening exploits. The last week had been spent with her nose to the loam, planting small black seeds that should have been planted after Christmas. For one whole week, she had been rendered inarticulate and exhausted with her mind turned somewhat cabbage-like, but she was excited about her mother visiting in June, not least to have a maternal presence to help with the overwhelming domestic chores.

The first half of May began on a sunny, positive note. On the 1st, Ted Hughes wrote to Aurelia and Warren Plath that Devon had been enjoying Cape Cod weather. Sylvia, he said, was finally brown and tanned and he could not recall ever seeing her so happy. The cherry trees and daffodils had all burst into bloom and the peach tree beneath Plath's study window had five blossoms. Ruth Fainlight and Alan Sillitoe arrived on the 2nd in time to enjoy Court Green as it came alive in the spring. On the 4th, Plath wrote to her mother that the latest batch of visitors were no trouble at all since they pitched in with cooking and washing up and entertaining themselves. Most importantly, Plath was still able to get time in her study during the mornings. It was during this visit that Plath read her poem 'Elm' to Fainlight, who praised it so much that Plath subsequently dedicated the piece to her. In 2013, Fainlight would stand on the stage at The Royal

Festival Hall in London reading 'Elm' aloud to celebrate 50 years of the *Ariel* poems.

The first half of May appeared to be taken up with visitors, neighbours, and gardening. Plath wrote no poetry at all. On the 7th, she enjoyed lunch with Elizabeth Sigmund and later that day attended a farewell dinner for the Tyrers at The Burton Arms. There were further visits to Mrs Hamilton across the road at Crispins, and on 16 May Nurse Winifred Davies took Plath to visit Mrs Kathleen Macnamara who lived nearby in Cadbury House, a grand sprawling former vicarage. Kathleen's husband, Terence Macnamara, worked in television for ITV and during the week stayed in a London flat. Mrs Macnamara, who could no longer face living in the city, moved to Devon and the plan was for the couple to retire there eventually. Plath was shown around the large, impressive house and took afternoon tea there. Two days earlier, Plath wrote to her mother saying she was swamped by domestic tasks and described the laburnum, lilac, and 'thundery purple' bluebells in the garden. Nicholas, for some inexplicable reason, had been crying at night and this had left Plath weary and not wanting to 'do a thing'. But in anticipation of her mother's visit, requests were lodged for certain items she might be able to 'squeeze' into her luggage, such as Plath and Hughes's fishing rods, their Victrola[11] and aniseed flavouring for making springerole.[12]

Somewhat tired and run-down, it is likely Plath was in no mood to host yet more guests on the weekend of 18 May. David and Assia Wevill, who had taken over the Chalcot Square lease from Plath and Hughes, were due to arrive on the Friday evening, and they were to be shortly followed by Hughes's parents and Uncle Walter. Plath stated firmly that she would be glad when it was all over.

There has been much written about the weekend visit of the Wevills in all of Plath's biographies. It seems any attempt to try and accurately sum up this weekend relies on conjecture, gossip, and stories told long after the event. Biographies explore the possibility that Assia Wevill travelled to Devon with the express purpose of seducing Ted Hughes, and that while she was there sexual tension between herself and Hughes was evident. Other reports claim Plath picked up on this attraction and acted appallingly, insisting that the Wevills depart early. Interestingly, one person who was present at the weekend, David Wevill, has given his own account, stating he recalls a perfectly pleasant weekend, with Plath charming company and he and Assia departing on the day scheduled. He did note Plath's nerviness and is quoted in *Bitter Fame* as stating that often a look of terror would pass across her face as though she was having the most terrible thoughts. But he liked Plath and found her good company. He did not detect anything amiss during the stay in Court Green.

Bitter Fame offers the most detailed account of this weekend with some curiously insightful details. Stevenson describes the meals, the evening talks, listening to a Robert Lowell recording, and a walk on Dartmoor. She even depicts a scene of Plath and Assia Wevill weeding onions together in the garden. During this incident, Plath realises that Wevill's feelings for her third husband, David, appeared to be on the wane. This is interesting for there can be no other source for this insight than Plath's own depiction of the scene describing her thoughts and reactions. This suggests that either Stevenson or the co-author of the biography, Olwyn Hughes, had access to, or memories of, Plath's 'missing' journal. Equally, in letters held by The British Library, Olwyn Hughes writes that Plath's manuscript of *Double Exposure* contains a blow by blow account of the Wevills' stay at Court Green. Writing *Birthday Letters* years later, Ted Hughes admits in the poem 'Dreamers' that it took only one night with Assia Wevill in the house for the dreamer in him to fall in love with her.

With Plath's voice from this time oddly silenced, all we have are the retrospective writings of Ted Hughes and the creative output of Plath via her poetry. However, as previously stated, it is rather dangerous to read poetry as straight autobiography unless it presents itself as such (e.g. *Birthday Letters*). It does appear that poems written by Plath at this time begin to deal with some uncomfortable subjects—distrust, cruelty, and apprehensions—but equally it is arguable whether they are any more unsettling than poems written the previous month such as 'Elm'. This suggests the possibility that the Plath–Hughes marriage was already under some strain before the arrival of the Wevills. Certainly, in fragments of the surviving journal notes, Plath's irritation with Hughes at certain moments is evident, as is her distrust. From Hughes's point of view, in his poem 'The Lodger', he describes a psychosomatic heart problem that appeared to begin the month after the move to Court Green. A classic symptom of anxiety, Hughes became convinced he was dying of heart disease.

Plath's poetical themes of the previous month—the drudging housewife of 'An Appearance' and the narrator of 'Elm', who claims 'Love is a shadow/How you lie and cry after it', are picked up and amplified in the poems she wrote after the Wevills' visit. 'The Rabbit Catcher' (21 May) deals with the suffocating constriction of a dangerous relationship with a sadistic husband. On the same day, 'Event' makes the doomed claim that a relationship has become so broken and mistrustful ('I cannot see your eyes' 1990: 192) that ultimately 'Love cannot come here' (1990: 195). Perhaps more tellingly, there is a long gap of three weeks before Plath writes to her mother. Of course, during this time she was busy hosting Hughes's family, writing more poems, and gardening. However, it was very rare during all of Plath's lifetime that she left such a long gap between writing home.

Two days after her visit, Assia Wevill mailed Plath a thank you letter which included a piece of tapestry complete with thread in response to Plath expressing a desire to take up needlepoint. The intricate rose design was started by Plath and it even features as one of her calendar 'to do' tasks on 29 May, but she did not finish it. Months after Plath's death when Elizabeth Sigmund was living at Court Green, she received a letter from Ted Hughes asking her to search Plath's desk and remove anything 'incriminating' against him, in anticipation of a visit from Mrs Plath that summer. What Sigmund did find was the letter and tapestry from Wevill stuffed into the side drawer of a desk. Retrieving it, Sigmund completed the needlework as a point of defiance. Over the years it crumbled and disintegrated into nothing. The letter from Wevill is now held in The British Library. The signature 'Assia' is written in pencil and the letter has clearly been folded twice long ways. Written on the underside in Assia's hand, also in pencil, but in large capital letters and underlined, is the word 'SYLVIA'.

On 25 May, Plath began work on another unsettling poem, 'Apprehensions', musing upon a changing scenario of different coloured walls and corresponding emotions: white, grey, red, and black. The narrator asks a desperate question, 'Is there no way out of the mind?' and the poem finishes with menacing imagery as 'Cold blanks approach us' (1990: 196). It took Plath three days to finish this poem, completing a final typescript on the 28th. This was the last poem she wrote for over a month.

Towards the end of May, Hughes's parents and Uncle Walter arrived in Devon for a six day visit, with the male guests staying at The Burton Arms, and Mrs Hughes staying in the guest room at Court Green. The following month, Edith Hughes would write to Aurelia Plath that they had enjoyed an immensely happy visit and that Plath was looking extremely well. The children had been good and Court Green was full of old world charm with a somewhat unruly garden. Seemingly, if any tensions were present within the Plath–Hughes marriage, they had not been on display during the family visit.

Saturday, 2 June on Plath's wall calendar is marked with a star—indicating a special day. She had sent a telegram the day before to America congratulating her brother Warren on his wedding. Having organised the shipment of a rose-coloured blanket bought in Exeter, but coincidentally made in Mytholmroyd, Yorkshire, Hughes's birth town, Plath hoped the new couple would like their present. Certainly Plath felt sad missing her brother's wedding day and even considered right up until the last minute splashing all of her last savings on a plane ticket to America. The rest of the week in Devon was quiet. No poems, no writing and by 7 June, the first letter to her mother in over three weeks, Plath wrote that she had taken time off from her study and engaged in three days of gardening. Although in this letter she asked for forgiveness for her silence, she explained it was 'partly' to do with the number of visitors throughout May. She did not offer what the other reasons were. Interestingly, the only visitors who were described as no 'strain' were the Sillitoes, implying that the Wevills and the Hugheses were more demanding, although she does write warmly about her in-laws.

The same day that Plath wrote this letter, two other significant events occurred. The first was Plath's decision, upon the advice of Winifred Davies, to take up beekeeping. The local beekeeper, Charlie Pollard, held a meeting that evening in his garden on Mill Lane where Plath was introduced to the art of beekeeping. This would inspire, four months later, her startling sequence of bee poems. The second event was the news that Plath's neighbour, Percy Key, was dying. The slow demise of her neighbour coupled with her new hobby of beekeeping, must surely have brought back memories of her own father, Otto Plath, an expert on bees and a man who died slowly from diabetes mellitus when Plath was eight.

If Plath was feeling disturbed by these events, she showed no sign when Al Alvarez visited the following day on his way to Cornwall for a rock-climbing holiday. He found Plath cheerful, confident, and playing the perfect host showing him around Court Green. Hughes, he noticed, was much quieter and happy to let Plath take the lead, a change from the time he had known them in London. Later that evening, Plath returned to Charlie Pollard's house to collect an old hive which she planned to paint in anticipation of the arrival of her bees.

Between 8–20 June, Plath spent her time visiting neighbours, arranging new work with the BBC, and preparing for her mother's arrival on the 21st. On 9 June she wrote to the Kanes apologising for her silence and explaining that her time had been taken up with gardening and beekeeping. The next day, Plath and Hughes drove to Winkleigh to have tea with the Billyealds whom they met at the bee meeting. Plath's thoughts and observations about the Billyealds' lives, home, and stories are recorded in minute detail in her journal notes from 1962. On the 11th, Plath wrote an interesting letter to her old professor and colleague at Smith College, Alfred Fisher, asking if she could buy some pink Smith memorandum paper as she had developed a 'fetish' for it.[13] In fact, during her year teaching at Smith, Plath had taken from the store cupboard reams of this paper to use for her writing. It then appeared to become her good luck talisman for producing work. Anyone who has spent time in the archives at Smith College cannot fail to be moved by Plath's *Ariel* poems handwritten and typed on this bright pink paper.[14] In contrast, it is noticeable that Plath's final poems composed in London are on stark, white, blank paper, much 'deader' than the swirls and flourishes on the pink background. Whether Fisher complied with Plath's request is unknown.

Three days later, George Macbeth wrote to Plath accepting her poem, 'The Surgeon at 2 a.m.', and asking her to read a Carolyn Kizer poem, 'The Great Blue Heron', for a BBC broadcast called *The Weird Ones*. The following day, Plath also submitted a short opinion piece called 'A Comparison', discussing the difference between writing poetry and prose. She requested that she record this for the programme, *A Poet's View of Novel Writing*, on the 26th of that month when she would be in London. On the 15th, she wrote the final letter to her mother before her impending visit, with no hint of any discord at Court Green:

> I have been working so hard physically out in the garden that I am inarticulate and ready for bed by evening, hence my long silences. I don't know when I've been so happy or felt so well. (1988: 457)

She also excitedly informed her mother that they had just officially become beekeepers. The old hive had been painted white and green and now housed some docile, Italian hybrid bees. The following day was a two-starred day on the calendar indicating Plath and Hughes's sixth wedding anniversary. If they celebrated at all it is not recorded. Tasks for the day included weeding the garden, planting seeds, painting, altering Frieda's dress hems, and studying German.

Around 18 June, Plath wrote to Olwyn Hughes and included a picture of Nicholas. Finally, Plath claimed, she felt as though she were pulling out of three years of maternity 'cow-push' and was finding the time in her study a poultice. Domestic tasks, however, were relentless. In the run up to Aurelia Plath's arrival, much cleaning and painting took place at Court Green. Following 21 June, it becomes more difficult to piece together Plath's movements as the regular letters home to her mother obviously cease and there are few poems. Certain details can be read in letters Plath wrote to friends, but there are gaps and silences. The day after her mother arrived, Plath wrote to the Kanes, seemingly to help them to find a cottage in the West Country. In this letter she wryly reports the dramatic arrival of her mother at North Tawton Station. As Plath and Hughes were walking across the railway bridge, they saw the London train pulling away from the platform shortly followed by Aurelia Plath leaping from the moving train with her luggage and twisting her ankle as she landed.

Within three days of Aurelia Plath's arrival, Plath and Hughes left for a trip to London. They learned that on 25 June, their neighbour Percy Key had died. Arriving back from the city, Plath viewed Percy's body, lying in his coffin, in the cottage next door to Court Green. Once again, Plath's X-ray vision took in every aspect to record in her journal: the colour of the coffin, Percy's jaw propped shut with a book, the sheets flying clean and sweet in the sun. These details sat briefly in Plath's imagination along with Percy's funeral and burial in a nearby cemetery off Exeter Street in the town. Then on 28 June, and over the next two days, Plath wrote 'Berck-Plage'. This extraordinary poem fuses the death of Percy Key with a visit the previous summer to Berck-Plage on the Normandy coast, a seaside town filled with hospitals and sanatoriums. Mutilated war victims and sick people took their exercise on the sands there. The beach was scattered with old concrete bunkers, gun turrets, and other relics from the war. What is especially fascinating about this poem is that the early drafts reveal that Plath intended to include a third theme in the poem—the birth of Nicholas. Thus there is the contrast of the elderly dying man, the birth of new life, and the recovery of damaged life on the beach sands in France. At some point, Plath decided to remove the reference to childbirth, which alters the theme of the poem somewhat, removing the imagery of hope. Indeed the narrator bluntly states that 'the sky pours into the hole' of the open grave—'There is no hope, it is given up' (1990: 201). It is interesting to note that Plath began writing this poem *before* Percy Key's funeral, so her decision to include so much detail about his service and burial could well have informed her decision to remove the reference to Nicholas's birth. Equally, the drafts show that she was struggling with the childbirth section, the imagery not quite working or in keeping with the rest of the developing poem. While Plath was working on this piece she was going about her daily business. On 28 June, she hosted a lunch for Elizabeth Sigmund, serving spaghetti, salad and a lemon pie. Elizabeth recalls that Plath never spoke about what she was writing. Her friendship with Elizabeth was based on other interests—politics, music, cooking and gardening.

Throughout the month of June, Plath worked hard to get her poems out and in publication. She submitted four pieces to *The New Yorker*, six to the BBC, and a further six to *The Observer*. Of these, only 'The Rabbit Catcher' and 'The Moon and the Yew Tree' were accepted for broadcast by the BBC. *The Observer* accepted 'Event' and 'The Rabbit Catcher'. Although a later recording exists of Plath reading 'The Rabbit Catcher', if she ever did make a recording of 'The Moon and the Yew Tree' it is now, sadly, lost.[15] On 30 June, the same day she finished 'Berck-Plage', Plath's recording of 'A Comparison' was broadcast over the BBC and no doubt listened to in Devon by a proud Aurelia Plath.

On 1 July, Plath's wall calendar includes a reminder to work on her novel. Which novel this actually was, remains in some doubt. It is not until the following month that she instructs herself to start work on *The Interminable Loaf* (which would become *Double Exposure*), so this was either the novel Aurelia Plath described as a continuation of *The Bell Jar* story, or it was preliminary notes and sketches for *The Interminable Loaf*. Olwyn Hughes recalls that one chapter of this 'missing' novel contains an account of the Wevills' visit in May. Another chapter includes an account of the 'Plath' and 'Hughes's characters travelling on a trip to London in June when their marriage was going wrong. This means it is feasible that Plath's early work in July was related to planning these chapters for what would become *Double Exposure*.

Throughout July, Plath would write only three poems. The first, around 2 July, was 'The Other', a disturbing account in which the narrator appears to refer to infidelity and illicit fornications that 'circle a womb of marble'. This repeated assertion of barrenness is a theme that from this point on recurs throughout Plath's work and her personal letters. The women that Ted Hughes became involved with are, according to Plath, all barren. This belief of Plath's is interesting and certainly Elizabeth Sigmund recalls that Plath was especially proud of being the bearer of Hughes's children. It was important to her that he was the father, and she felt certain that none of the women he subsequently became involved with in her lifetime intended to have children with him. Given that Assia Wevill became pregnant just before Plath's death (and subsequently had an abortion), Sigmund believes that if Plath had knowledge of this pregnancy it would have upset her greatly. 'The Other' was originally titled 'Mannequin', which was crossed out but evidently stayed within Plath's consciousness to reappear the following year in her poem 'The Munich Mannequins'. Early versions of the 'The Other' are clearly addressed to a black-haired rival who flexes her silks and is gloved to the elbow carrying seven small corpses in her handbag. This rival squats on the narrator's pillow, 'stealing' fornications and deranging everything.

The following day, Plath travelled to London to meet with George Macbeth of the BBC and to lunch with Douglas Cleverdon. This seems to have been just a day trip, but interestingly it was around this date that Ted Hughes first contacted Wevill, according to the poet Nathaniel Tarn.[16] In the meantime, life at Court Green and Aurelia Plath's summer vacation continued. Visits were made to a variety of neighbours, and on 6 July, Plath and Hughes drove to Elizabeth Sigmund's house to join her in celebrating her birthday. Sigmund recalls Plath arriving with a bottle of wine and a cake wrapped in a shawl. She appeared bubbly and happy, although other guests at the house noticed that Hughes was quiet and sullen.

Three days later, on 9 July, underlying tensions within the Plath–Hughes marriage exploded to the surface. Travelling for a day out in Exeter with her mother, Plath declared how happy she was, but Aurelia Plath held suspicions that all was not well. After shopping and eating lunch, the two women decided to return early to Court Green, and as they walked into the house, the phone began ringing. Plath picked up the receiver just as Hughes appeared at the top of the stairs. On the other end of the telephone, a woman pretended to adopt a man's voice and asked to speak to Hughes. Plath immediately recognised Wevill's voice and handed the receiver to her husband. When the phone call was over, Plath tore the telephone wire from the wall. What followed this incident can only be pieced together from a letter Aurelia Plath wrote to her son Warren, and from external sources who became part of the unfolding drama. Hughes caught a train to London that day, likely thrown out by Plath. Unable to face an empty bed that night, Plath left Frieda with her mother and drove with Nicholas to Elizabeth Sigmund's. She arrived in a highly distressed state as documented by Sigmund in her memoir. The following day, as Plath returned to Court Green, according to Nathaniel Tarn, Ted Hughes arrived at the Wevills' armed with four bottles of champagne claiming it was his birthday and he wanted to celebrate. In fact, Hughes's birthday was not until August.

Clearly trying to pull herself together, Plath, on the following day, (11th) wrote 'Words heard by accident, over the phone.' In this poem, the narrator hears devastating words which 'plop like mud' onto the phone table, leaving it irredeemably dirty and stained. On the same day, she wrote to her friend Clarissa Roche urging her to come and stay as she felt 'homesick' for her. On this day back in London, Nathaniel Tarn notes that Hughes and Wevill spent the day together, ending the evening in the pub with Al Alvarez. Hughes then stayed the night with Alvarez in his flat. Two days later on the 12th, Hughes and Wevill met in a hotel and spent the whole day in their room. That evening, Hughes decided to return to Devon, and Wevill accompanied him to Waterloo Station. Back in Chalcot Square, somehow hearing what was occurring, a distraught David Wevill set out for Waterloo armed with a knife. Unable to find Hughes he returned to the flat and took an overdose of pills. When Assia Wevill returned and found him, she called an ambulance. On the way to the hospital she told him that Hughes had raped her.

It is difficult to imagine what the atmosphere must have been like when Hughes arrived back at Court Green, but it took only three days for Aurelia

Plath to move out and stay with Winifred Davies for the rest of her time in North Tawton. Writing to Warren Plath on 17 July, Mrs Plath gave some insight into what was occurring. Although her first week there had been one of the happiest in many years, she subsequently noticed a number of events that gave rise to tension and therefore felt that moving out was the best option. Ted, she claimed, wanted her to stay. What is curious about this letter is Aurelia Plath's opinion that the problems in the marriage were 'not new', but had been made 'afresh' by recent incidents. She believed Plath had taken on too much 'again'. On the day Aurelia moved out of Court Green, Plath once again turned to Elizabeth Sigmund, driving to see her with toys and piano music to share.

In the week that Hughes returned from London, Plath wrote no poems or letters. Her calendar remains empty apart from opening some new bank accounts in Okehampton and taking tea with Mrs Macnamara. It does not contain her usual menus or cooking schedule. On 19 July, Plath took herself on a day trip to London for a meeting with the Arts Council, but the following day was back in her study. The 20th saw her produce the poem 'Poppies in July', a muse upon the desire for the numbness of opiates. Early drafts of this poem contain startling and violent imagery, the poppies seemingly taking on the characteristics of the speaker and described as being like a mouth left by a fist 'smashed with bad news'.

On 21 July, Plath made contact with the Irish poet Richard Murphy to inform him that he had won first prize in the Cheltenham Poetry Contest of which Plath was a judge. She congratulated him and asked if it would be possible for her and Hughes to stay with him in Ireland for a well-needed holiday. On the same day, Plath sent three new poems to Alvarez at *The Observer*, asking him to be honest and hoping he might take one or two as she was in need of money. By the 23rd, Plath had returned to see Elizabeth Sigmund, this time taking with her a typewriter, a sweater, and casserole.

Sometime around the end of the month—very possibly 25 July—Plath held the first of her bonfires upon which she burnt letters and papers from Hughes's study, photographs and letters from her mother and, according to Aurelia Plath, the manuscript of her second novel intended as a birthday present for Hughes. The following day, Plath and Hughes took a pre-arranged trip together to Bangor in Wales for a Poetry Conference and reading connected with the journal *The Critical Quarterly*. On the way to Bangor, a visit was made to their friends Daniel and Helga Huws, who were made aware of the marriage problems. Back in London during this time, Assia Wevill informed Nathaniel Tarn that Hughes would 'probably stay with his wife'.

The beginning of August appeared to be a quiet time. Plath's calendar shows she had an evening appointment in a nearby village, Hatherleigh, on the 2nd, which according to Elizabeth Sigmund could possibly have been a poetry reading she gave to support a local arts group to help them raise money for a new meeting hall. On 4 August, Aurelia Plath left Devon to return to America. In *Letters Home* she wrote:

> When I left on August 4, 1962, the four of them were together, waiting for my train to pull out of the station. The two parents were watching me stonily—Nick was the only one with a smile. It was the last time I saw Sylvia. (1988: 458)

Just three days after her mother left, Plath made an appointment with Sparkes Solicitors in Crediton. It seems likely that she was taking advice on a legal separation for less than two weeks later she writes to her mother that this is her intention. On 9 August, Plath travelled to London for the day where she recorded 'The Surgeon at 2 a.m.' for the BBC and met the Kanes. Clearly, a conversation took place between her and the Kanes regarding their accommodation difficulties. Struggling to pay the rent, it seemed as though they were being threatened with eviction. At some stage Plath suggested that they were welcome to stay at Court Green rent-free in the guest room, if they were willing to help out with the children and around the house. Hughes's whereabouts at this time are unknown, although certainly towards the end of the month, Plath wrote that he was spending his week in London but returning to Court Green for weekends. Perhaps Plath's offer to the Kanes was to help secure some support for herself as well as them. It seems likely that Hughes was in Devon on the 9th, as after returning from London on the 10th, Plath wrote to the Kanes informing them that Hughes would drive them back to North Tawton the following week. Also on 10 August, Plath's Letts calendar contains just three words 'Start Int. Loaf!!!'—a reminder to herself to seriously start work on her novel. Whether this was the day she began, we cannot know for sure.

There was just one poem written in August, on the 13th (started on the 12th), 'Burning the Letters', narrating the uneasy secrets that papers and correspondence can hold. Clearly based on Plath's own clearing out of Hughes's attic study and the bonfires Aurelia Plath witnessed, the narrator in this poem is tortured by 'the eyes and times of postmarks' (1990: 204) on envelopes, which leave her tired and strung up. A striking moment in the poem occurs when, fanning the flames, the narrator sees wilting at her foot 'a name with black edges' (1990: 205), while in the distance a fox is torn apart by a pack of dogs.[17] 'Burning the Letters' covers twenty pages in draft form. Beginning as an untitled poem, it is partially composed on the verso of Hughes's 'The Thought Fox'. Initial ideas in draft clarify certain points in the published version. In draft form, the name that wilts at the narrator's foot is that of a girl. The early versions are addressed directly to another person, the narrator uses the term 'you'. It would seem Plath toyed and played with ideas and imagery in this poem. There is, however, something unique about the manuscript. This is the only draft in the archive which contains doodles and pictures by Plath. On page seventeen, she has drawn a happy looking owl sitting on a perch and a cat smiling beneath an upside-down heart.

The same day that Plath finished this poem, the Kanes arrived to stay at Court Green. They would remain there for just over two weeks. They took charge of the children while Plath and Hughes travelled to London on the 15th. This trip was to meet Sylvia's benefactor and friend, Olive Higgins Prouty, who put them up in The Connaught Hotel. They spent the evening drinking cocktails and watching Agatha Christie's *The Mousetrap*, followed by breakfast in bed the next morning. Although Plath and Hughes presented a united front, Plath wondered whether Prouty had been suspicious during that meeting since she made certain comments over dinner about unfaithful men.

By 17 August, back in Devon, Plath wrote again to Richard Murphy, further arranging to visit him in Cleggan on the west coast of Ireland. On the same day she wrote to her mother that the Kanes were staying and the house was a mess, but she was looking forward to a new woman, Mrs Bires, who would help with the children, starting the following week. Plath also told her mother that the doctor's wife, Joan Webb, was going to organise a horse-riding instructor so Plath could begin lessons. This is one of the significant moments when the domestic and the professional merge, as some of the most powerful *Ariel* poems are based either on the experience of horse riding or using horse imagery. Plath's first lesson was taken with Miss Redwood at Lower Corscombe stables in Sticklepath on 27 August.

The rest of the month was spent quietly, visiting friends, cooking, and cleaning the house. Plath saw Elizabeth Sigmund three times during the final two weeks of August, taking her potatoes and onions from the garden at Court Green. During these weeks, no doubt run-down and feeling the strain, Plath became sick with influenza. In a 27 August letter to her mother, she wrote that Kathy Kane's help had been invaluable in looking after the babies while Plath recovered. This suggests that Hughes was not around and indeed she informed her mother that he spent most of the week in London. Feeling that she was leading a degraded life, waiting for him to come home, she had decided upon a legal separation.

From this point onwards, Plath's letters become difficult and unsettling to read as the marriage deteriorates further and accusations are made. Hughes's letters, too, make unpleasant claims about Plath as he informs family and friends that the marriage is over. In an undated letter held by The British Library (but clearly written during the summer upheaval), Hughes wrote to his sister Olwyn that he regarded his marriage, house, and Sylvia as the dead end of everything. The marriage, he claimed, was fine up to a point for the first two years, and after that steadily worse. He wanted to live alone, to be free to do what he wanted, see who he wanted, and to travel. He also claimed in this letter that over the last six years he had repressed 10,000 desires in a gentlemanly way and now that he had given vent to them he was insatiable. His plan was to live in Germany until he could speak fluent German, then Italy until he could speak fluent Italian, and so on. Towards the end of the letter he acknowledged his children stating Nicholas was a stranger to him, but leaving Frieda would be more of a problem. Plath, he claimed, had helped bring this decision about because she did not want him near Court Green due to his 'sinfulness'. Dealing retrospectively with letters written during such an emotionally disruptive time is difficult, and in fairness to Hughes, despite what he claims here, after Plath's death he did take charge of their children and developed a deep and loving relationship with both his son and daughter.

Plath's main concern towards the end of August was for her children. She wrote to her mother that she felt willing to put up with just about anything to give the babies a stable home, but ultimately believed the father that Hughes had become was worse than a totally absent father. She regarded him as a selfish liar and an adulterer. However, she did state that he had it in him to be kind and loving, he just chose not to be. The situation, she claimed, had wrecked her writing, her sleep, and her health.

In the breakdown of any relationship, emotive and harsh words are spoken. In the case of Plath and Hughes, their words are forever preserved, as though the hurt and heartache is suspended in time, never to be resolved. The poems in *Ariel* and *Birthday Letters* make the Plath–Hughes marriage endlessly accessible, perpetually raw. While this may seem negative, what it did produce was some of Plath's most astounding work. Had the story ended in a different way, perhaps some of these poems would have lost their immediacy, but with Plath's early death, this was never going to be the case. Perhaps what is more important about these *Ariel* poems is that we hear Plath's voice in the way that she wanted it presented. This was her creative declaration made both on paper and through her final recordings. Other representations of her voice, such as the 'missing' novel, have now been 'lost', which makes what we do have all the more precious. Placing these poems in their historical context shows how unique they were, and remain. That strong, angry, yet controlled female voice denouncing men and the state of marriage, pre-dates second-wave feminism, yet is concerned with many of the issues that would ultimately spark the movement. Plath, of course, was not a feminist, and there has been much speculation as to whether the movement would have drawn her in had she lived. Perhaps the more important point to be made is that Plath's poems since the 1960s have offered women (and men) a voice with which they can identify, a voice which is a source of strength.

The beginning of September saw Plath ill once again with influenza, and running a temperature of 103 degrees. A proposed meeting in London with Eric White[18] had to be cancelled due to her sickness, and even on the 5th in a letter Plath wrote to the Kanes, she was still feeling very weak. After two weeks of living at Court Green, the Kanes, uncomfortable with the crumbling marriage, moved out; Plath was eager to find child care for when she visited Ireland. In this letter she assured the Kanes that she had employed a nanny so they did not have to disrupt their own plans to help her out. Three days later, Plath wrote two more letters. The first to Richard Murphy which confirmed final details of the visit to Cleggan, and the second to Elizabeth Sigmund complaining about the Kanes who seemed unable to cope with the children, and informing Elizabeth of her plans for Ireland. This letter wistfully showed Plath longing to see Elizabeth and planning a visit when she returned from holiday to bring fresh vegetables from Court Green's garden.

On Tuesday 11 September, Plath and Hughes left for Holyhead to catch the ferry across to Dublin. Later, after this visit was over, Plath admitted that she had gone hoping something might be salvaged from the marriage. What she could not know was that even before they had left, Hughes had secretly arranged to leave her there alone and meet Assia Wevill in Spain. Nathaniel Tarn's diary contains detailed information of this plan related to him by Assia Wevill, who herself was holidaying in Canada. She spent the last ten days of this holiday in Spain with Hughes, a plan unknown to her husband. Even fifty years later in 2012, when the biographer Carl Rollyson approached David Wevill with this information, he was staggered to learn that it had happened. Hughes, to cover his tracks, had pre-arranged for a friend in London to send Plath a telegram bearing a London stamp stating that he would be returning to Devon soon. However, all of this was unknown to Plath as they crossed the Irish Sea to spend their first night in Dublin, eating oysters with a fellow poet-friend from Boston, Jack Sweeney and his wife Maire. The following day, Plath and Hughes headed to Cleggan via Galway to meet Richard Murphy and stay as guests in his cottage, 'The Old Forge'. Cleggan, a small fishing village on the west coast of Ireland, is approached across empty and brown peat moors. The harbour is lined with lobster pots and fishing nets. Gulls swoop perpetually.

The Old Forge is a small stone-built building, renovated by Richard Murphy himself from what used to be the blacksmith's forge in the village. As you enter the front door, a short passage leads to a small, basic bathroom at the end of the hall. Two doors off to the right of the passage lead into bedrooms just large enough for a double bed or twin beds. Plath and Hughes were to stay in one of these rooms sleeping in twin beds of Spanish walnut. A door off to the left of the hallway leads into an open plan living room with a kitchen on the far wall and a beautiful, green Connemara marble fireplace on the right wall for peat fires. Open stairs on the left run up to another much larger bedroom, the only room upstairs, in the eaves of the cottage. An account of Plath's stay here is contained in an appendix by Richard Murphy in *Bitter Fame* and in his own autobiography *The Kick*. He recalls taking Plath and Hughes sailing on his boat the *Ave Marie* across to Inishboffin Island, and drinking beer in Day's Hotel. He also tells of a visit to Yeats's Tower and Coole Park, as well as calling in at his own ancestral home, Milford, on the border of County Mayo. It was during Plath's time here that she was introduced to Kitty Marriot, a local woman, with whom she arranged to rent a house for the winter. The cottage, called 'Glasthule', in nearby Moyard overlooks a lough and brown, rolling hills. Behind the house is an ancient monument. Kitty Marriot, who lived in the cottage next door, milked her own tuberculin-tested cows and offered to help Plath with the children. It was just what Plath needed, she felt, to winter in a smaller, manageable house, somewhere away from bad memories where she could work on her novel and regain her health.

The Old Forge, Cleggan. Plath stayed here as the guest of Richard Murphy in September 1962. (*Gail Crowther*)

According to Richard Murphy, during supper on the Saturday night of their visit, Plath provocatively rubbed her leg against his under the table, which he interpreted as her making a move on him. Elizabeth Sigmund finds this unlikely, since before Plath left for Ireland she clearly stated she was staying with a 'gay poet' (Murphy discusses his sexuality very poignantly in *The Kick*). However, others present at the dinner, Hughes and poet Thomas Kinsella visiting from Dublin, appeared not to notice this drama unfolding. Neither, it would seem, did Plath. The following morning, while Murphy was out working, Hughes left Cleggan informing Plath that he was going to visit his friend, the artist Barry Cooke, in County Clare. He assured her he would return to Cleggan in time for their journey home the following Tuesday. Hughes immediately left to travel to Spain and had no intention of returning. Finding this situation when he returned from work, Murphy appeared to panic, and insisted that despite having been abandoned by her husband, Plath should return to Dublin that day with Thomas Kinsella. Under no circumstances could Plath remain in his home unchaperoned. Somewhat bewildered and distraught, Plath did return to Dublin and spent two tearful days with Thomas and Eleanor Kinsella who showed her great kindness.

Returning to Court Green alone and unaware of her husband's whereabouts left Plath in a terrible state. When Elizabeth Sigmund saw her she was appalled. At some stage between the 19–21 September, Hughes's pre-arranged telegram arrived. Whether Plath found out about his whereabouts in Spain at this time is unknown (certainly she found out later), but on one of these nights, she fled to the home of Winifred Davies in a highly distressed state. What occurred during those hours is recounted in a letter from Davies to Aurelia Plath.[19] Plath, it seemed, had realised that Hughes had no intention of returning, and had therefore definitely decided upon separation. Davies felt worried that Plath was facing a 'hard hill to pull', but ultimately was convinced it would be better for the children to have one happy parent than two arguing ones. Although she acknowledged only having one side of the story, Davies does criticise Hughes in this letter, accusing him of not accepting his responsibilities or taking his fair share in the practical side of the marriage such as paying bills, sorting taxes, etc. This was an astute observation by Davies, since Hughes's letter to his sister Olwyn, cites exactly these emotions—how he wants to be free from the restrictions of marriage and children and be able to do what he wants when he wants.

On 21 September, Plath wrote to Richard Murphy sending him her unused train ticket from Galway to Dublin (she had returned by car with Thomas Kinsella) and asked him not to resent her wintering in Ireland. She planned to finish her novel while at Glasthule and he would not have to see her unless he wished to. The same day, perhaps trying to maintain some control, she called her solicitor in London to make an appointment, and then went horse riding at Lower Corscombe. The rest of the week was spent visiting Elizabeth Sigmund and writing letters to her mother, keeping her updated on the situation. Finally, on the 25th, she took a trip to London having arranged for a nanny, Miss Cartwright, to stay with the children. The letters Plath wrote at this time are difficult to read. Clearly hurting and struggling to come to terms with the situation, Plath raged against Hughes and her mother and complained about suffering mysterious temperatures which the Doctor refused to treat. Trying to hold the house together, she got kittens for the children from Mrs Macnamara and called them Tiger-Piker and Skunky-Bunks.

While in London, Plath visited Mr Charles Mazillus of Harris, Chetham & Co. Solicitors at 23 Bentinck Street W1. Here she discussed instigating a legal separation from Hughes, and here, according to a later letter to her brother Warren, she took her first cigarette and began smoking. This aspect of Plath's distress Elizabeth Sigmund found particularly disturbing since prior to this, Plath had always been highly critical of smokers, and indeed admonished Elizabeth on a visit when she had accidentally left her cigarettes within reach of Frieda.

During the rest of September, Plath wrote letters to various family and friends informing them of her marriage break-up. On the 26th, she wrote to her mother that her solicitor was busy trying to locate Hughes. He had not been in contact with Plath since leaving her in Cleggan, and she was desperately trying to gain control of her life. To the Kanes she wrote arranging a visit to see them and trying to organise a reading job with Marvin. Another letter on the same day informed Olive Higgins Prouty of Ted's desertion and her plans to spend the winter in Ireland. Interestingly, in this letter she claimed that from 5 a.m. each morning she had been working on her novel which she hoped to have finished by mid-winter.

Three days later in another letter to her mother, Plath again mentioned her novel but said she was finding it very difficult to concentrate.

At the end of September, Plath produced two poems, both reflecting the situation unfolding around her. The first, written on the 26th, was 'For A Fatherless Son'. It is difficult not to read this poem as highly autobiographical given what is written on the manuscript of the poem. The subtitle is 'To A Deserted One' and it is dedicated to 'N.F.H', Plath's son. The second poem written on the 30th, a month before Plath's thirtieth birthday, is 'A Birthday Present'. The drafts of this poem show it began with a title 'A Poem On Her 30th Birthday'. What is remarkable reading this draft is how seamlessly this poem wrote itself. There are very few strike-throughs or alterations, as though the dam had finally broken and the words began to flood. This, in fact, is exactly what did happen. Over the next thirty days, Plath would write twenty-five poems.

The first of these poems, 'The Detective', was produced on 1 October, which, like 'A Birthday Present', almost appeared to write itself. There are few changes from the first draft, although Plath did appear to struggle with the mouth imagery in the sixth stanza. In particular the line 'To wrinkle and dry' (1990: 209) was worked and re-worked. The poem relates some terrible event that has occurred but gone initially unnoticed ('What was she doing when it blew in' 1990: 208) until the lies and deceits shake out, producing a disastrous effect on the maternalised body of the narrator. The smiling man of the poem vaporises the woman, the children, the home, and the whole estate. There is no body to be found, there is no death:

> There is only the moon embalmed in phosphorus.
> There is only a crow in a tree... (1990: 209)

On this day in London, Assia Wevill phoned Nathaniel Tarn to talk about her ten days in Spain with Hughes. She explained how this secret meeting had been arranged as early as August. Wevill also told Tarn how well she and Hughes worked together and that they were planning to write a film script.

Back in Devon on the following day, Plath produced another poem, 'The Courage of Shutting-Up' (initially called 'The Courage of Quietness'), a reflection on the difficulties of keeping the mouth shut when it is loaded with accusations:

... with accounts of bastardies.
Bastardies, usages, desertions and doubleness, (1990: 210)

The following day began a long series of poems, which Plath would refer to as her Bee Sequence, recounting her new hobby of beekeeping. On 3 October she wrote 'The Bee Meeting', on the 4th, 'The Arrival of the Bee Box', on the 6th, 'Stings', on the 7th, 'The Swarm', and on the 8th she began 'Wintering' which was completed the following day. Within just six days she had produced five poems depicting that first meeting in Charlie Pollard's garden in June through to the delivery of her Italian hybrid bees. Interestingly, as this sequence progresses, the bees appear to become more than just bees. They are used to symbolise other political and emotional states. They can search out lies ('Stings') and the bees are all women ('Wintering'). The final poem in the sequence ends on a note of hope and was the poem Plath chose to close her version of *Ariel*, which she left ready for publication at the time of her death. In 'Wintering' the future of the bees, the garden, the flowers, comes under question as winter closes in:

Will the hive survive, will the gladiolas
Succeed in banking their fires
To enter another year?
What will they taste of the Christmas roses?
The bees are flying. They taste the spring. (1990: 219)

On a more literal level, Plath's hive did survive the winter. In a letter Winifred Davies wrote to Aurelia Plath in the May after Plath's death, she informed her that she now owned Plath's bees. During December 1962 when Plath was arranging her affairs to leave Devon, she packed her bees tightly and left them in the care of Winifred Davies. The terrible winter of 1962–63 set in, the Big Freeze, and Plath would die in the February. During the terrible snow storms, the roof blew off Plath's hive in Davies' garden. But come spring, when Davies went to check on the bees they were still alive because Plath and had wrapped and packed them so preciously.

During the week that Plath was engaged in writing her bee poems, she also attended a musical concert in Hatherleigh Church with Elizabeth Sigmund. On 7 October she wrote again to Richard Murphy in Ireland and told him she was getting a divorce. Since she was due to take up residency in Moyard, just down the road from Cleggan, she wanted reassurance that he would not resent her being there.

On 9 October, there is a noticeable change in Plath. The tempo of her life suddenly increased rapidly. It seems likely that around this time, Ted Hughes arrived back at Court Green. Assia Wevill had gone to Germany with her husband and so Hughes decided to leave London and return to Devon. The page on Plath's Letts calendar for this week has been removed. However, on the 9th a jittery Plath wrote to her mother that a storm had broken a window at Court Green during the night and she was so frightened that she had called the police. Having heard about David Wevill chasing Hughes to Waterloo Station armed with a knife, she appeared worried that Wevill would come after her and the children. For the first time, she informed her mother that she was getting a divorce, reasoning that if she was divorced Hughes could never be unfaithful to her again. She would be able to start a new life, she just needed money.[20] Here Plath's anxiety becomes palpable. Hughes had agreed to pay £1,000 per year for the children, but Plath worried that his family would oppose this; she worried her own family (specifically her Aunt Dot who was a strict Catholic) would disown her because of the divorce; and she worried about having to face going to court. All these emotions rushed out in the letter while she described Hughes walking around the house humming to himself, in love. Nevertheless she had no intention of returning to America:

> If I start running now I will never stop. I shall hear of Ted all my life, of his success, his genius ... I must make a life all my own as fast as I can ... the flesh has dropped from my bones. But I am a fighter. (1988: 465)

On 10 and 11 October, Plath wrote 'A Secret' and 'The Applicant'. The former deals with the taunting superiority of one who holds a secret, and the latter is a biting critique of marriage and the position of women. Perhaps mindful of the need to generate more income, Plath also submitted eight poems to *The New Yorker* and ten poems to the *Hudson Review*. On 11 October, Ted Hughes left Court Green and his marriage, on the same day that Assia Wevill informed Nathaniel Tarn that she was to be named as co-respondent in the Plath–Hughes divorce. At some stage either before or just after Hughes left on the 11th, Plath wrote one of her most well-known poems, 'Daddy', famously depicting a Nazi father figure and sadistic vampire husband. Whether Plath was genuinely relieved to be free of Hughes, or whether she was demonstrating bravado is difficult to know, but her letters the following day show how much better and happier she felt knowing that Hughes had gone. 'It is *over*. My life can begin...' (1988: 466). She informed her mother:

> Every morning, when my sleeping pill wears off, I am up about five, in my study with coffee writing like mad—have managed a poem a day before breakfast. All book poems. Terrific stuff, as if domesticity had choked me. (1988: 466)

To her brother Warren, she believed herself to be a very funny novelist and that she hoped to have her book finished by Christmas.

A short break occurred in Plath's writing over the next couple of days as she drove to St Ives in Cornwall to pay a visit to the Kanes, who were now living in 'Quaintways', a small cottage in a cobbled courtyard. A creative account of these days can be found in the poem 'Lesbos', which Plath completed four days later. This visit was important to Plath and she regarded it as the first of many necessary independent acts that she would have to get used to. Upon her return to Court Green, Plath wrote 'Medusa' on the 16th and two frantic letters to her mother on the same day. Given the subject material of the poem, the leech-like, touching and sucking maternal figure, it is perhaps easy to imagine some of the tensions Plath felt towards her mother. While on the one hand, Plath disliked her tremulous, tearful worry, on the other hand, she needed her mother as her *confidante*, a role which Aurelia Plath had always played throughout her daughter's life. However, given what her mother had seen that summer, Plath did not want to see her again until the horror had subsided. Wildly, she asked for Warren's new wife, Margaret, to fly over and be with her. She was terrified, she needed someone from home; she felt very alone.

These letters written on 16 October reveal Plath to be in a terrible state. This is confirmed by Elizabeth Sigmund who recalls the vast amount of weight Plath had lost over the summer (almost two stones) and her hacking smoker's cough. Once again sick with influenza, fevers, and a temperature of 101 degrees, Plath's letters launch into a tirade against Hughes and the Hughes family. She informed her mother that she had written to Edith Hughes of 'Ted's desertion' as she could no longer stand the cheery letters. It is at this point that Plath's relationship with her in-laws began to break down as she became convinced they would not support her in receiving maintenance for the children. Other than her general wild distress and sickness, it is quite difficult to pinpoint exactly why Plath believed this. With no existing letters from the Hughes family to Plath, we can only piece together evidence from incomplete correspondence. Certainly she interpreted a later letter from both Hughes's mother and Aunt Hilda as implying she could look after herself. This seemed to be in response to comments they made that she was lucky with two children to be able to work from home. Over-sensitive and over-wrought, Plath took this as meaning that she should earn her own money. It would seem this was not the attitude of Edith Hughes. A letter from her to Olwyn Hughes held in The British Library, undated but clearly written about this time, shows how bewildered Hughes's parents were about the situation and about their son's behaviour. Ted Hughes came in for harsh words from his mother, who was upset that he had treated his wife and children so badly. She wrote that she understood if he wanted to leave the marriage, but he should not have gone about it in the way that he did. These sentiments are echoed on 17 October when Edith Hughes wrote to Aurelia Plath about how shattered she was by events and that she would always 'be there for Sylvia'. In fact Edith Hughes is highly complementary of Plath, referring to her as a brilliant woman and a brilliant broadcaster who was famous in her own right. Full of regret over the marriage breakdown, she closed her letter saying that she was convinced that if Plath and Hughes had stayed together, there was nothing they could not have achieved.

Plath, of course, was not privy to these letters. Frightened, sick, and with a high temperature, her worst fears seemed to become reality as she struggled to cope with loneliness. On 16 October she wrote, 'I am fighting now hard against the odds and alone' (1988: 469). The only outlet in which Plath appeared fully in control was her poetry. On the 17th, she produced the brilliantly defiant poem 'The Jailer', and on the 18th, 'Lesbos'.

It was on the 18th that Plath's tone and mood changed once more. In a flurry of three long letters, the first one to her mother, she showed a more upbeat and positive attitude. Seemingly this had been brought about by the help of Winifred Davies who had managed to secure a nanny to help Plath with the children. Susan O'Neill Roe, aged twenty-two, who lived with her parents in the nearby village of Belstone, agreed to spend the day at Court Green between the hours of 8.30 a.m. to 6 p.m. The difference this made to Plath's life was immeasurable. However, one unchanging theme of these letters was Plath's anger towards Hughes. His hate, venom, and sadism, she wrote to her mother, would be commemorated in her next novel. In a letter written the same day to Olive Higgins Prouty, Plath again reiterated Hughes's sadism and her eagerness to begin a new life. To her brother Warren, she claimed to be up and writing from 4 to 8 a.m. each day. Hughes, she claimed, had set her life back by at least a year.

What Hughes was thinking at this time is not really known. His selected *Letters* have a gap between September and December 1962, and the poems in *Birthday Letters* are more oblique, drawing on myth and religious imagery. A letter from late September to his sister reveals Hughes was annoyed that Plath had been trying to locate his whereabouts by employing what he referred to as 'snoops'. He felt sure that as long as he could keep giving her cash there would be no problem. Ultimately, he concluded she would have to grow up. It would do her no harm. Three months later in a letter to his brother Gerald, Hughes wrote of his relief at escaping the relationship. Although in many ways he found Plath to be the most gifted woman, he finally found marriage to her impossible.

From mid-to-late October, more poems flowed out of Plath daily. On the 19th, 'Stopped Dead', on the 20th, 'Fever 103', and on the 21st, 'Lyonnesse' and 'Amnesiac'. During this time Plath also wrote letters to friends and family. On the 19th she asked Clarissa Roche to visit and informed her of the impending divorce. On the 21st she expressed annoyance to her mother that Hughes had dumped and abandoned her in the country. What she really needed at some stage in the future was a London flat and a live-in nanny:

I dearly love the people I know in town, but they are no life. I am itching for museums, language study, intellectual and artistic friends (1988: 473).

Still eager to get her new poems published, she submitted seven to *The New Yorker* on 22 October, but only one, 'Amnesiac', would eventually be accepted. More professional engagements came her way from London, and Plath wrote that she had been invited to present the American Night at the Poetry Festival in The Royal Court Theatre the following July. In this same letter to her mother, she apologised about her grumpy and sick letters of the previous weeks, blaming her illness and fevers. Everything had started to look much brighter. The local villagers liked her, she was writing furiously, Susan O' Neill Roe was like a younger sister, and exciting work prospects were coming her way. The following day, on the 24th, Plath wrote 'Cut', 'By Candlelight', and 'Nick and the Candlestick'.[21] These poems were followed the next day by 'The Tour' and another large batch of letters keeping friends and family up to date. To her mother she wrote of an up and coming trip to London where she intended to attend the PEN party and record 'Berck-Plage' for the BBC. She informed her brother wistfully that she kept his wedding picture on her writing desk. To Olive Higgins Prouty she described the peacefulness of her study and the vase of late poppies and blue cornflowers in front of her as she wrote. These flowers would feature prominently in a poem written at dawn two days later on her birthday, 'Poppies in October':

> Oh my God what am I
> That these late mouths should cry open
> In a forest of frost, in a dawn of cornflowers. (1990: 240)

On the same day, Plath wrote the title poem of her second collection, *Ariel*, having informed her mother that she would be spending her birthday riding her favourite horse (Ariel) at the stables in Lower Corscombe. What Plath could not know at this time was that various family and friends were corresponding with each other regarding Plath's decision to winter in Ireland. Evidently at some stage in October, Aurelia Plath wrote to Olive Higgins Prouty voicing her concern about her daughter's plan, and seemingly urging Prouty to talk her out of it. On 27 October, Prouty replied to Mrs Plath in full agreement and described the Ireland trip as a 'bad idea', at which point she sent her opinions to Plath. In the meantime, Plath travelled to London for a two day visit. On the 29th, she recorded

'Berck-Plage' for the BBC and met Al Alvarez at his flat in the afternoon to read her new poems and drink whisky. In the evening she attended the PEN party at Glebe Place. It was during this literary event that she boldly informed everyone that she was divorcing Hughes. It was also at this event that Daniel Huws saw Plath for the last time. He recalls saying goodbye after the party with a kiss on the cheek, and putting her in a taxi.

The following day, Plath lunched with Peter Orr of The British Council and in the afternoon gave a radio interview, reading some of her newest poems such as 'Daddy', 'The Applicant', and 'A Birthday Present'. What is quite extraordinary is that it was only the day before this recording that she finished writing 'Purdah' and 'Lady Lazarus', both of which she felt confident enough to read during the interview.

These final days of October saw Plath submitting more new work to various publications. Two batches were sent to *The New Yorker*, five on the 26th and a further three on the 30th. On 31 October, she submitted four poems to *The London Magazine*. In all, this month Plath submitted

Plath's horse riding view from the stables above Lower Corscombe where she would ride Ariel. 'The blue pour and tor of distances.'(*Gail Crowther*)

thirty-nine of her new poems. Only three were accepted.[22] Whether or not her trip to London reminded Plath of the vibrant cultural life she felt she could build there, by the end of October she had decided not to spend the winter in Ireland, but to move back to London instead. Certainly, if both her mother and Olive Higgins Prouty were urging her to do this, they may have had some influence. Back in North Tawton, Winifred Davies had already made her opinions clear—Plath should sell Court Green and move closer to London.

On 1 November, Plath attended a film society meeting with Susan O'Neill Roe and her mother Nan Jenkins in the Town Hall at North Tawton. Bringing a bit of culture to the country, Plath told Mrs Prouty that they had watched a 'foreign movie'. In the same letter, she recounted the 'difficult' time at the PEN party in London the previous week, making it known to friends and work contacts that she was divorcing Hughes. Using a striking piece of imagery, Plath described how she was writing her poems in the Blitz with bombs exploding all around her.

At the beginning of November, those women around Plath in whom she was confiding were also reporting back to Aurelia Plath. Whether Plath was aware of this is not known, but certainly she suspected that to be the case with Winifred Davies. Whether this limited what Plath felt she could speak about is hard to know. On 3 November, Winifred Davies wrote to Aurelia Plath expressing her relief that the Ireland plans were now off. Olive Higgins Prouty also wrote to Mrs Plath with advice to pass onto Plath's solicitor in London. She again re-iterated her disapproval of the Ireland plans. While these women were a vital source of support for Plath, after her death when Hughes discovered their letters he was infuriated by what he saw as their interference. 'Night-Ride on Ariel' from *Birthday Letters* accuses them of playing a role in Plath's suicide as they dragged her this way and that with their words and advice. From Plath's point of view, their letters, support, and advice were a lifeline as she struggled in her country isolation.

On 3 November, Plath began to transform herself. She visited a hairdressing salon in the nearby village of Winkleigh recommended to her by Joan Webb. Here Plath had her hair cut, leaving it long at the back and curling around her face in a fringe. This, along with some new clothes she bought in Exeter with money sent by Mrs Prouty, helped with her confidence. She felt attractive once again and noticed that men in the street paid her attention. When she next saw Hughes in London later that month, he did not recognise her. Also on the 3rd, Plath began writing two poems, 'Getting There' and 'Gulliver'. The first of these deals with a disturbing train clattering towards some terrible destination, with imagery reminiscent of the Nazi round up of Jews:

The train is dragging itself, it is screaming—
An animal
Insane for the destination... (1990: 249)

Both of these poems would be typed up into a final version three days later on 6th November while Plath was in London, flat-hunting. Before leaving for the city, she wrote another three poems on the 4th: 'The Couriers', 'The Night Dances', and 'Thalidomide'. The latter two poems contrast sharply. 'The Night Dances' is a tender poem written to Nicholas recounting a ritual dance he would carry out in his cot each evening before falling asleep. In comparison, 'Thalidomide' deals with the horrific birth defects that began to emerge in the 1960s from the eponymous drug given to pregnant women for excessive morning sickness. The more politicised nature of this poem suggests a possible direction in which Plath may have taken her poetry had she lived longer and become more involved in increasing social movements that sprang into life during the mid-1960s. Certainly this was the case with some of her contemporaries such as Robert Lowell and W. S. Merwin.

Between 5 and 7 November, leaving the children with Susan O'Neill Roe, Plath went to London in search of a flat for the winter. She stayed with friends Suzette and Helda Macedo in Hampstead and while there, on the 6th, typed up final versions of 'Getting There', 'The Night Dances', and 'Gulliver'. Writing to her mother on the 7th in an ecstatic tone, Plath believed that she had found the perfect flat in Fitzroy Road, Primrose Hill, in a house where Yeats had lived as a boy. Furthermore, her second volume of poems was almost finished and she intended to dedicate it to Frieda and Nicholas. When her novel was finished, she hoped to dedicate it to Olive Higgins Prouty. Her third volume of poetry, when completed, would be dedicated to her mother. She claimed finally to feel free and happy and credited most of this to her work. She felt her life was so much fuller and richer than Hughes's, and those around her expressed their shock at how little jealousy or vengefulness she showed towards him. It is possible at this stage that Plath did see a way forward, a new life in London with her work and her babies and perhaps even at some stage sharing that with someone sympathetic to and supportive of her work. Carl Rollyson's book *American Isis* contains an interview with Al Alvarez who claims that Plath was 'in love' with him at this time following an incident that occurred between them towards the end of October. But with incomplete correspondence, 'missing' journals and Alvarez understandably refusing to explain further, we cannot know if this informed any of Plath's decisions.[23] It is, of course, also possible to see a certain amount of bravado in this letter. Less than a month since Hughes had left Court Green, Plath faced the immense challenge of moving herself and the children to London, and arranging the upkeep of Court Green over winter while trying to write enough to earn a decent income. All of this without immediate family support.

Back in Devon, while Plath waited to hear whether her application for Fitzroy Road had been successful, she had dinner with neighbours in Court Green, invited friends for afternoon tea, and continued to write poems. On the 8th, she corrected the final typescript for 'Thalidomide'. On the 11th, she wrote 'Letter in November', and on the 12th started writing 'Death & Co', bringing it to completion on the 14th. On the 13th, between this writing spell, she randomly opened her copy of Yeats's *Collected Plays* with Susan O'Neill Roe to playfully see if he would give her a message about the flat application. The words to which she pointed were from *The Unicorn from the Stars* and read:

> Go then, get food and drink, whatever is wanted to give you strength and courage; gather your people together here; bring them all in. We have a great thing to do. I have to begin ... I want to tell it to the whole world. Bring them in, bring them in, I will make the house ready. (1953: 347)

Plath, in her black ink underlined these words and wrote, 'The prophecy—true?'

On the 16th, Plath wrote 'Years' and 'The Fearful', the latter taking as its inspiration the phone call from Assia Wevill in which she pretended to be a man. At this point, Plath's writing began to slow down, as though the pistons that had been driving her for the last six weeks were finally running out of steam. She sent a batch of poems to *The Atlantic*, and in keeping with other editors of the time, Peter Davison in Boston found them to be 'alarming'.

The following day, Clarissa Roche arrived for a visit to Court Green. Plath told her tales of the ritualistic fire burnings she had been carrying out over the summer, describing how she swept hair, nail trimmings, and skin from Hughes's study and chanted an invocation as they were thrown into the flames. Plath also told Roche that she felt sure someone had placed a curse on her and that the 'vibrations' of the curse seemed to centre around the living room. Half-jokingly, she claimed to have looked up the chimney to see if a witchcraft doll had been stashed up there (it had not) and she asked Clarissa to look too. These conversations appeared to unnerve Roche, who found Court Green old and creaky and believed it to be almost certainly haunted. When she left, she continued to worry about Plath living there on her own through the autumn and winter of 1962.

The final two poems written in November were 'Mary's Song' (started on the 18th and finished the following day) along with 'Winter Trees' on the 26th. Between writing these poems, Plath attended dinners with her neighbours, went shopping for more new clothes, and caught yet another cold. On the 19th she wrote to her mother that her second volume of poetry was now finished:

> Well, I have finished a second book of poems in this last month—30 new poems—and the minute I get a mother's helper in London, I will do novel after novel. (1988: 480)

On the 20th, she wrote to Olive Higgins Prouty that she had many novels in her crying to be written. These letters almost quiver with Plath's creativity, as though having to suppress all of this work was somewhat agonising for her. Despite her assurance earlier in the month that she was glad to be free of Hughes, her anger towards him erupted again in a letter on 22 November. She claimed to despise him and wanted him to have nothing to do with either her or the children. Part of this anger may have sprung from her discovery that he was now involved with another woman, Susan Moore (née Alliston), and that this woman wanted to meet her.[24] Indeed

Susan Alliston wrote just one week before Plath's death asking if they could meet. At this stage in November, Plath was firmly of the opinion that it would be a pleasure Alliston would most definitely have to forego.

By the end of the month, having heard that her application for Fitzroy Road had been successful, Plath wrote a final letter to her mother from Devon:

> I can't wait. I have been culture-starved so long, utterly alone, that these last weeks are a torture of impatience. (1988: 482)

She had arranged with a local removal man, recommended by Winifred Davies, to move her things to London. Her last days in Devon were spent hosting farewell dinners and packing. Two final Devon poems were written on 1 December, 'Brasilia' and 'Childless Woman'. On the following day Plath began 'Sheep in Fog', although this would not be finished until a month later in London. Her final horse riding lesson took place on the first day of the month just before Plath travelled to London for four days to finalise the flat details between 3 and 6 December. While there she signed the five year lease on the flat, held meetings about further possible work for the BBC, and marvelled at the thick white fog that shrouded the city for her entire stay. It also seems likely that a significant meeting with Hughes took place while she was there (Crowther and Steinberg, 2013).

The British Library holds a number of books filled with draft poems written by Ted Hughes, some of which would end up in *Birthday Letters*, others which he abandoned. In a school book titled 'That Sunday Night,' Hughes, in an untitled poem, recounts an incident which he appears to place in London in December 1962. During this undated evening, he and Plath are guests at a restaurant in Dean Street, Soho called L'Epicure.[25] He recalls that they were there at the request of 'Eric', very likely their mutual friend Eric White. Evidently, all parties got drunk throughout the evening and upon departing the restaurant, Hughes asked Plath where she was staying and where the children were. He questioned how many times they walked around Soho Square saying the same things and eventually, according to Hughes's account, Plath asked if she could return with Hughes to Dido Merwin's flat where he was staying, and again they walked around the Square.[26] Hughes finally agreed to let her return with him, where the tirade continued. He hoped she would fall sleep but it went on and on until the neighbours downstairs banged on the ceiling. The next morning, reported Hughes, things were much calmer between them and they departed as 'cold-mouthed' as 'flood victims' who were travelling towards the same morgue.

Cross checking these possible dates against what we know of Plath's movements that December in 1962, it seems most likely that this poem refers to this London visit Plath made at the start of the month. Certainly it was before her permanent move there on 10 December, otherwise Hughes would not have needed to ask where she was staying. Plath's calendar for that year shows a visit to London on Monday 3 December, followed by a meeting in a restaurant in Leicester Square the following day to discuss a possible reading to be given in Stevenage. Plath was certainly home in Devon by Thursday the 6th as an unpublished letter from Aurelia Plath (dated 8 December) states how much she enjoyed their phone conversation the previous Thursday evening.[27] This means the night that Hughes writes about was either on Monday 3rd, Tuesday 4th or Wednesday 5th December. Rather cryptically, Plath's calendar shows a crossing out for Tuesday December 4th. She initially wrote something which was then scribbled over in ink. Although the odd letter is legible, the entire entry is not, and it would be interesting to know if this referred to any event that took place in London.

Leaving herself only four days to pack, Plath returned to Devon on the 7th, managed to squeeze in a final hair appointment on the 8th, and then spent the rest of her time sorting clothes for herself and the children, stringing her onions, packing apples, potatoes, honey, and holly and arranging care for the two kittens. Her excitement at returning to London was evident in all of the letters she wrote. Many of her friends and work contacts were there, she would be able to get regular work with the BBC, host a salon in her flat, send the children to good schools and enjoy what she had craved throughout her time in the country—a 'cultural' life. Court Green would be her summer home where she would return each year in time for the daffodils and the cherry blossom. One week before her death, Plath wrote a letter to Elizabeth Sigmund telling her of London life and her plans to return to Court Green in the spring. 'Thank God you will be there', Plath exclaimed. In the meantime, a whole new life was opening up, exciting and full of hope. Plath told her mother that she was the happiest woman alive:

> I am so happy and full of fun and ideas and love. I shall be a marvellous mother and regret nothing. I have two beautiful children and the chance, after this hard, tight year, of a fine career—schools and London in winter, Court Green, daffodils, horse riding and the beautiful beaches for the children in summer. (1988: 478)

On Monday 10 December, Sylvia Plath's time in Devon came to end as she closed up the house for winter and drove to London. It was a fine, clear, crisp, blue day.

Appendix

A Poem, A Friend

Gail Crowther with Elizabeth Sigmund

In mental life nothing which has once been formed can perish, everything is somehow preserved and in suitable circumstances it can once more be brought to light.

(Freud, quoted in Thurschwell, 2000: 4)

Introduction: 'The painted wooden face was known to me....'

A poem can hold many meanings for both the writer and the reader. Who can say with any certainty what forces may be at work when a poet puts pen to paper and a reader then consumes what is written. There is so much space, so much room for interpretation, unconscious resonances, instinctual needs and desires. If, as Freud states above, nothing which has once been formed in our mental life can ever perish, then it becomes almost unimaginable to consider the storehouse of memories we must bring to the writing and reading of any text.

In this appendix we aim to explore the unconscious processes that may be at play in a poem. 'Shep-en-Mut', written by Elizabeth Sigmund, is on the surface a beautiful poem about an Egyptian Songstress, Priestess of Thebes and Bearer of the Little Milk Jar. It is about encountering the ornately decorated and mummified body of Shep-en-Mut in a museum exhibition and being struck by something uncannily familiar in the unfamiliar. Yet it could also easily be a poem about Elizabeth's friend, Sylvia Plath, who perhaps acts as a silent, ghostly presence, informing the poem. By analysing the lines of verse and exploring how Elizabeth's memories and stories may have informed the poem, we are able to offer a possible reading of both a poem and a friend.

However, we offer you a warning: this is not literary criticism or a traditional memoir. Rather, we invite you to join us as we explore words, memories, and stories; as we follow the labyrinthine path of poems and people, and play.

For Robert Young, author of *Untying the Text*, the very act of writing becomes limitless in its own playfulness. In other words, when we encounter a text we do not necessarily have to search for an essential 'truth', but rather we can drift and disentangle; writing is to be 'ranged' over. A text, then, is something which is woven together from ideas, memories, and conscious and unconscious instincts and desires. As readers, we encounter this text, involve ourselves in some playful textual analysis, and may well become 'undone, like a spider that comes to dissolve itself in its own web' (Young 1987: 39).

In *Image Music Text*, Roland Barthes, too, claims that encountering a text can result in a multiplicity of meanings; it is the language that speaks, not the author, and if we follow a text it can be 'run (like the thread of a stocking) at every point and at every level' (1977:147).

In this sense, faced with a poem, any poem, we can allow ourselves to range over the possibility of interpretations and not prescribe ourselves to some mythical unity of meaning. This does not mean, of course, that a poem cannot be sparked by a particular event, but simply that once written, to give the text a singular meaning is to close the writing and limit its readings. Therefore, as we consider the poem 'Shep-en-Mut', it is worth bearing in mind that the poem was inspired by a particular visit to a museum. Elizabeth recalls:

In the 1970s I took my children to the museum in Exeter to find information about hut circles on Dartmoor. While we were looking at exhibits I noticed a painted wooden mummy case, standing in the sunlight of a window. I have never been particularly interested in Egyptology, and was amazed to feel something deep inside me responding to this image: I said 'Hello,' as if suddenly meeting an old friend.

I went to the information desk and found a leaflet about the mummy. She was Shep-en-Mut, a priestess in Thebes, and she was described as a 'songstress of Amun Re'. I borrowed a friend's ticket for the library at Exeter University and made copious notes of Egyptian funerary rites.

It seems there was something about the backlit figure of Shep-en-Mut standing in the sun that drew Elizabeth's attention. A resonance perhaps, or the unearthing of a buried memory. Elizabeth describes it as like 'meeting an old friend', despite never having had a particular interest in Egyptology prior to this visit. This feeling of the familiar in the unfamiliar is an example of Freud's idea of *unheimlich* ('the uncanny'): 'the uncanny is that class of the frightening which leads back to what is known of old and long familiar.'[1] Often the uncanny is connected to the return of the dead or the fear of spirits and ghosts. In this case we could argue that the uncanny is connected to the preserved body of the Egyptian Songstress, both somehow dead and strange, while at the same time not-dead and, in some indefinable form, striking a note of familiarity. Quite where this resonance and feeling of 'knowingness' came from occurred to Elizabeth when, after this visit, she put pen to paper and showed the resulting poem to her husband:

I wrote the poem and put it away in a drawer for some months, without giving it a further thought. When I showed my husband William the poem he said, 'What a sad and beautiful poem about Sylvia.' I protested at once; however, on rereading it I saw what he meant, and was amazed that I could not have known this myself.

Shep-en-Mut

The painted wooden face was known to me.
She stood in the dusty museum sun,
Painted eyes lengthened with kohl.
Azure, terra-cotta, white,
Emblazoned cartonnage.

The Isis wings, spread in care and love.
Curving protective Neckbet and Nepthys.
Beneath, the corticate skin,
Black bitumen. Eyeless, cracked and black,
Dessicated viscera, wrapped apart.

Leaving child and husband, moving through satin bands of shadow,
Singing in the ecstatic sun.
Feet hissing through the silken sand
She carried the Milk Jar and a Palm frond,
Worshipping and serving each day.

This lady was the songstress of Amun-Re,
Her songs curved upward in the great Temple of Thebes.
The stone beauty of the face of the God above her frailty
Gave her voice a scope of praise denied to our dessicated senses

When death stooped on her, claws and beak ripped.
Then feathers lay outstretched in love.
Horus wings, Night Heron beak,
Having slain, now standing guard in fearful phalanx.
Leaving the echo between the roof trees.

Her flesh must be pickled, cured with cinnamon and myrrh.
The skull, frail as a blown egg,
Emptied of its convolute majesty,
Stuffed with delicate resinous rags.
When the sucking natron has had its meal
Her shell will taste the shriving sun and wind once more.
Blow gently, shine kindly down, Amun-Re, on thy slave.

She shall be wrapped in fine linen
Layer on layer, and laced like a shoe.
The last we shall see in linen and plaster and paint.
May her journey be safe through the dark tunnels
May her soul sing in light before her God,

In soft peace. The holding wings enfold my friend.

Priestess of Thebes. Singer of Amun-Re
Bearer of the little Milk Jar.

Elizabeth Sigmund

We see here one possible reading of this poem by William Sigmund. A reading of which the writer, Elizabeth, was unaware. In *Sigmund Freud*, Pamela Thurschwell questions whether it is ever possible to approach a text and avoid examining the psychic motivations of the author. Not only is the act of reading unstable, but she argues that the author's intentions are never fully retrievable, not even to themselves. If this is truly the case, then it is by extension possible that an author's unconscious motives remain inaccessible *especially* to themselves. Elizabeth is certain when she wrote this poem that it was not about her friend, Sylvia Plath. Yet the more she read it and considered the associations, the more she began to feel that unconsciously her thoughts and memories of Plath in some way may have informed her writing of the poem. It is this play of hidden intentions and possibilities that encourage us in this appendix to see what may be retrievable in the writing of a poem.

'This lady was the songstress of Amun-Re....'

Throughout 'Shep-en-Mut' there are echoes of Plath's own work, such as the painted sarcophagus of 'Last Words'[2] and the little milk pitchers of 'Edge'.[3] But there are also resonances of Elizabeth's memories of Sylvia as a woman and a mother. When Elizabeth writes of Shep-en-Mut's 'emblazoned cartonnage', she describes the depiction of Isis with her wings spread in love and care. This brings to mind the importance to Plath of the Isis engraving she had hanging on her wall, and which she was photographed standing in front of holding her infant Frieda (see *Letters Home*, p. 357). Isis is the Egyptian Goddess of Motherhood and Children from whom all beginnings originate. Often she is depicted nursing her infant son, Horus, with her wings outstretched to protect him. It is this depiction of the loving mother that Elizabeth recalls about Plath, and that upon their first meeting they were both mothers and wives of writers:

> When I first met Sylvia Plath in March 1962, she was 29 and I was 33, married to a writer, David Compton. It was almost a year before she died. Her daughter Frieda was almost two years old, my son James was three years old, and Sylvia's son Nicholas was a month old. Sylvia and Ted had bought Court Green, a beautiful seventeenth-century thatched house in North Tawton, a tiny mill town near Okehampton on the edge of Dartmoor.

Isis print 'Oedipus Aegyptiacus, Isis' from a book illustration in *Oedipus Aegyptiacus* by Athanasius Kircher, published between 1652 and 1654.

It was this setting in Devon at both their homes where the friendship between Elizabeth and Sylvia developed as they discovered a mutual interest in politics, industry, gardening, and motherhood:

> She and I discussed the military and industrial links between Britain and the U.S., and she was very pleased that we agreed on so many political points. I introduced her to Mark Bonham Carter, the prospective Liberal parliamentary candidate for mid-Devon, and they became close friends. We also had other interests in common—the teachings of Carl Jung and the paediatric specialist, Dr Spock. Over the spring and summer we visited each other regularly, each delighting in having found a friend in Devon with so many things in common.

Elizabeth recalls Plath as being an affectionate mother and one who took parenthood seriously. She remembers one particular visit from Sylvia when sitting at the dinner table with Nicholas on her knee; Sylvia laughed about how greedy Nicholas could be. As Elizabeth served up the food, Nicholas followed the dishes with his eyes and Sylvia exclaimed, 'Look at him! Look at his greedy eyes!' and gave him a tight hug. It is this notion of the playful, loving mother that brings to mind the 'Isis wings spread in love and care'. The depiction of Shep-en-Mut as a protective woman and mother made Elizabeth wonder retrospectively to what extent her memories of Sylvia and her children informed this second stanza of the poem.

However, it is not only Plath as mother who is evoked in Elizabeth's poem, but also Plath as poet and writer. Shep-en-Mut is a 'songstress' whose voice has 'a scope of praise', singing songs which 'curved upwards' in the Temple of Thebes. There is something ethereal about her gift which is 'denied to our dessicated senses'. This powerful voice and mastery of words echoes the fierce, lyrical beauty of Plath's own poems. Despite Plath being curiously modest about her own writing (Elizabeth recalls Sylvia never spoke to her about her writing), at all stages of her career when she was living in Boston, London, and Devon, Plath recorded her poems. Recordings can be heard ranging from the early poems of *The Colossus* to those staggering, late *Ariel* poems. The 'voice' of the poems, and the poem as a song, became increasingly important to Plath. In a BBC interview with Peter Orr in October 1962, she expressed her excitement at the new move to record poets reading their own work:

ORR: Do you think this is an essential ingredient of a good poem, that it should be able to be read aloud effectively?

PLATH: Well, I do feel that now and I feel that this development of recording poems, of speaking poems at readings, of having records of poets, I think this is a wonderful thing. I'm very excited by it. In a sense, there's a return, isn't there, to the old role of the poet, which was to speak to a group of people, to come across.

ORR: Or to sing to a group?

PLATH: To sing to a group of people, exactly, exactly.[4]

Plath's reference to the ancient role of the bard as a singer is reflected in Shep-en-Mut's role as songstress with poems and songs as public performances, as voices with 'scope of praise'. But there were other readings too, less formal than the BBC, in which Plath exercised her voice. Elizabeth remembers:

She gave poetry readings for an arts group in Okehampton, a market town on the edge of the moor. She helped them to raise the money to buy an old building for an arts centre for the district, and they told me how fond they had become of her.

During her friendship with Plath, Elizabeth was not aware of the type of poems Plath was writing.[5] Nevertheless, Plath appeared to express her emotions openly to Elizabeth during her regular visits:

Ted went to stay with friends in London, and during the sad autumn, when Sylvia was living at Court Green without Ted, she came to visit more often.[6] She brought fruit, vegetables and honey from her garden. We had long discussions about her sense of loss and anger, but I had no idea of the amazing poetry that she was writing early every morning.

It was not until after her death and the publication of *Ariel* that Elizabeth was able to truly appreciate the 'scope' of her friend's voice. It is the strength of this voice, the idea of the poet as songstress, which seems to echo in the fourth stanza of 'Shep-en-Mut'.

When death 'stoops' on Shep-en-Mut, she leaves behind her husband and child and we see how 'her flesh must be pickled' and her body stuffed with 'delicate resinous rags'. The 'sucking natron' mummifies and preserves the body as she is wrapped in 'fine linen' beneath plaster and paint. Again, we can see echoes of Plath's own poem, 'Last Words', in which her speaker describes how she will be rolled up in bandages with her heart stored beneath her feet, wrapped in a neat parcel (*Collected Poems*, p. 172). Yet there is also something here about loss and death. The preservation of the lost loved one in some ways can be seen as an attempt to hold onto one who has gone; a reluctance to give up the body to the inevitable cycle of decay and disintegration.

Death rituals exist in many cultures and these rituals are often an attempt to ward off the physical process of death, whether by preservation of the body, removal of locks of hair from the corpse to plait into jewellery, or photographs taken post mortem as *momentum mori*. Hallam and Hockey discuss the material nature of death and the ways in which the living negotiate their loss. Objects can become relics of the dead and used as tools of mourning. Thus, attempting to preserve the dead in 'things' could be seen as an attempt to reanimate the one who is lost and gone in order to stabilize a sense of self suffering from loss. As Hallam and Hockey state:

> Material culture mediates our relationship with death and the dead; objects, images and practices, as well as places and spaces, call to mind or are made to remind us of the deaths of others. Material objects invoke the dead. (2001: 2)

It could, of course, be argued that nothing invokes the dead more than a preserved body, a body which has been lovingly pickled with 'cinnamon and myrrh' and carefully wrapped 'layer on layer'. After her death, Plath's body was taken to University College Hospital and then removed to Leverton & Son Funeral Director's in Mornington Crescent, where her body was embalmed and placed in an Oxford Coffin.[7] Retrospectively, Elizabeth wonders to what extent her description of Shep-en-Mut is informed by her knowledge of Plath's own embalmed body:

> Some weeks after Sylvia's death, Ted asked us if we would consider going to live at Court Green, his house in Devon. He said that he could not go back to

live there: 'The house is full of ghosts'. He decided to sell to it, and he needed people he trusted to look after it and show potential buyers around.

He also talked to me about his horror at the thought of Sylvia's hair rotting, and said that he had had her body embalmed. I found all this deeply disturbing, and felt great sadness. We decided that we must try to help him, and went to live at Court Green, until he eventually felt able to move back there with his children and sister Olwyn. We bought a cottage in the village and saw Ted and his family regularly.

Insomuch as Shep-en-Mut is preserved, however, there is also a feeling of letting go: 'May her journey be safe through these dark tunnels.' It is this letting go which becomes a crucial part of the process, or the 'work' of mourning. Freud argues that 'in mourning, time is needed for the command of reality-testing to be carried out' ([1917] 1995: 589), and after this passing of time, the mourner will eventually let go of the one who is lost. Upon moving into Court Green in the months after Plath's death, the loss appears to Elizabeth in small and curious ways:

> One of the most painful things about moving into Court Green was to discover a line of Sylvia's shoes in the bathroom. Shoes are so personal, and there was something horribly final about their presence.

As Elizabeth wishes Shep-en-Mut a safe journey, this could well be a hope she directs towards Sylvia. Six days before her death, Plath wrote to Elizabeth. Her final letter from London was full of plans. She had been asked to give a reading at the Round House in Camden; she was to appear on *The Critics*, a radio programme on the BBC; Frieda had been enrolled into a nearby nursery school; and Nicholas was to have an operation on his eye. Moreover, stating her plans to journey back to Devon in March in time for her daffodils, Sylvia exclaimed to Elizabeth, 'Thank God you will be there!' Yet here we see Elizabeth saying goodbye to her friend who left on a very different sort of journey.

> After receiving Sylvia's last letter to me, I felt much more confident that she had begun to recover from the breakup of her marriage. It was therefore a terrible shock to read the article by Al Alvarez in *The Observer* (17 February

1963) 'A Poet's Epitaph', with poems and a photograph of Sylvia and Frieda in front of the Isis poster. The poems, which were later published in *Ariel*, were terrible in the depth of suffering they revealed. In particular, the line from 'Edge': 'The moon has nothing to be sad about, / Staring from her hood of bone' stuck in my mind as a horrible image of something which I had always regarded as a powerful symbol of female power and maternal strength.

I felt, somewhat ambiguously, that here was a voice speaking from the depths for the anguish and terrors experienced by many women.

Shep-en-Mut the Songstress was preserved to startle and astound with a voice which held an unusual 'scope of praise'. Even after death, 'singing in the ecstatic sun', she emblazons her way in the dusty museum room where she has stood since 1897. Plath's words, too, were preserved to pierce and astonish the reader. Speaking 'from the depths', with her bold and unique voice, she knew that she was 'writing the best poems of my life; they will make my name' (*Letters Home* p. 468); poems that will ensure her voice continues to be heard.

Conclusion: 'The holding wings enfold my friend....'

In this appendix we have attempted to explore some of the ways in which memories and experiences may inform the writing of a poem, sometimes unconsciously. Given this, the claim to any 'truth' seems spurious; as Barthes states, we can only follow a text like 'a run in the thread of a stocking' (1977: 147). Surely that is the beauty of writing, the infinite number of possibilities that it can offer to us as both readers and writers. Perhaps thoughts of Sylvia did, in some indefinable way, inform the writing of Elizabeth's poem. Perhaps equally, they did not. The point is that poems are there to be ranged over; that is part of their power.

Years after Plath's death, Ted Hughes gave Elizabeth Sylvia's copy of Dylan Thomas's *Collected Poems*. In her annotations, Plath highlighted her belief of what poems should 'do' and her desire for their longevity.

Sylvia Plath's copy of Dylan Thomas. Not to be reproduced without permission. (*Elizabeth Sigmund/Gail Crowther*)

Elizabeth recalls:

> Sylvia had marked many passages, including the 'Note' in which he [Thomas] wrote '… These poems, with all their crudities, doubts and confusions, are written for the love of Man and in praise of God, and I'd be a damn' fool if they weren't.' The message she marked most strongly were the last lines of 'Poem in October':

> O may my heart's truth
> Still be sung
> On this high hill in a year's turning.

We can never say with any certainty to what extent Plath informed the enigmatic figure of Shep-en-Mut in Elizabeth's poem, yet there are undoubted parallels, intentional or not, between the two songstresses speaking their bold and fierce words.

For Elizabeth, reflecting years afterwards, she finds resonance in her last wishes for Shep-en-Mut and those she holds for Sylvia:

May her journey be safe through the dark tunnels
May her soul sing in light before her God,
In soft peace. The holding wings enfold my friend.

It is in these closing lines that we see the possible merging of a poem, a friend.

Note: A version of this appendix was first published in *Plath Profiles Interdisciplinary Journal*, Vol. 3, Indiana University, 2010.

Endnotes

Chapter 2

1. At this time, Elizabeth was married to the writer David Compton, however throughout this piece she will be referred to by her present name, Elizabeth Sigmund.
2. Unless otherwise stated, all letters quoted in this chapter are held in the Lilly Library at Indiana University.
3. Indeed many years later after Plath's death, Hughes believed this motte to be so special he built a writing shed over the site.
4. The departure and arrival dates for this trip are confirmed by Plath and Hughes's stamped passports, which are held at Emory University.
5. The poem is not accurately dated—all drafts simply state it was written at some stage in September.
6. Despite not being made clear in the published version of this poem, early drafts clearly show Plath was writing in a male narrative voice.
7. 'Wuthering Heights', 'Blackberrying', 'Finisterre', and 'The Surgeon at 2 a.m.' At this stage Plath had a First Reading Contract with *The New Yorker*, which meant she was contracted to send all her new poems to them first for consideration before submitting elsewhere.
8. Plath herself had experienced a miscarriage earlier that year in February 1961.

9. Al Alvarez was the poetry critic for *The Observer* and a friend of both Plath and Hughes. He recounted this story at the 75th Sylvia Plath Symposium held at Oxford University in 2007.

10. This contract, first established on 24 February 1961, stated that Plath should send all new poems to *The New Yorker* for first reading before attempting to publish elsewhere.

11. Victrola was a brand of gramophone.

12. Springerle is a German biscuit with an embossed design made by pressing biscuit dough with a patterned rolling pin.

13. With this letter, Plath included a sample page of the pink paper and a signed copy of *The Colossus*.

14. Most of the *Ariel* poems on this paper are written on the verso of early drafts of *The Bell Jar*, with the exception of 'Poppies in October' and 'Ariel' which are written on fresh pages.

15. The reader for this BBC production, however, was not Plath herself but Cecile Chevreau, as indicated on Plath's typescripts for these poems now held at the University of Liverpool.

16. Nathaniel Tarn was a close friend of Assia Wevill. His diary notes are held at Stanford University.

17. Furthermore, Hughes's poem 'Epiphany' from *Birthday Letters* correlates the failure of his marriage with his failure to take care of a fox cub offered to him.

18. Eric White was a musician, poet, artist, and friend of Plath and Hughes, based in London.

19. Held in Lilly Library at Indiana University.

20. When Plath's probate was published on 22 May 1963, the full value of her effects (which went solely to Edward James Hughes, writer) was £2,147 4s 2d. This information was obtained from files held in Ancestry.com.

21. *Collected Poems* dates 'Nick and the Candlestick' four days later on the 29th, but the drafts clearly show this was written earlier.

22. These three were 'Amnesiac' by *The New Yorker* and 'Stopped Dead' and 'The Applicant' by *The London Magazine*.

23. The Alvarez papers in The British Library contain an illuminated copy of 'Ariel', hand-written and decorated by Plath and dedicated to Alvarez. An early typescript of 'Letter in November' also reveals

Plath dedicated this poem to Alvarez. Often these dedications did not get published when Plath's work appeared posthumously. Another example is 'Poppies in October', which was dedicated in typescript to Suzette and Helda Macedo.

24. In a startling coincidence, Susan Alliston was married to Clem Moore, who had been Warren Plath's room-mate at Harvard in the 1950s.

25. Although Hughes states L'Epicure was on Dean Street, it was in fact located on the corner of Frith and Romilly Street, close by to Dean Street.

26. Dido Merwin was the wife of the poet W. S. Merwin, friends of Plath and Hughes. Her flat was located at 17 Montagu Square, London W1.

27. This letter, dated 8 December 1962, is located in the Plath archives in the Mortimer Rare Book Room, Smith College.

Appendix

1. 'The Uncanny', an essay by Sigmund Freud, was first published in 1919. The full text can be accessed at http://people.emich.edu/acoykenda/uncanny1.html.

2. See 'Last Words' in *Collected Poems* (1981: 172).

3. See 'Edge' in *Collected Poems* (1981: 272).

4. A full transcription of this interview can be accessed at http://www.sylviaplath.de/plath/orrinterview.html where this citation is found.

5. Elizabeth did not even know that *The Bell Jar* was to be dedicated to her until after its publication. Plath wrote the news in her final letter to Elizabeth in February 1963. Elizabeth recalls that this letter was the only time Plath actually mentioned what she was writing: 'She said that we appeared in her new novel about life in North Tawton in which we appeared as plaster saints. Not flattering, I fear.'

6. Some, but not all, of these visits between Elizabeth and Sylvia were captured on Plath's 1962 Letts Calendar. The ones listed are 17 April, 7 May, 28 June, 16 July, 23 July, 22 August, 29 August, and 22 September. There were other visits and Elizabeth remembers that they organised outings too: 'We tried to cheer Sylvia with various outings, one was to a concert of early baroque music; she was amazed at the raw rich sound, but most of all by the strange names of the

instruments—viola da gamba, rebeq, bowed psaltery, etc.'

7. On 15 February after Plath's inquest at St Pancras Coroner's Court, her body was transported by rail from King's Cross, London up to Hebden Bridge in West Yorkshire for her funeral on the 18th. Warren Plath wrote to his mother on 20 February 1963 that there was a short service in the chapel of a funeral home in Hebden Bridge before the funeral party travelled to Heptonstall Church for another service and the burial. He described the service as simple and beautiful. It is worth noting that the date of Plath's funeral appears to be contested. While most sources state 16 February, notices in various U.S. newspapers do give 18 February as a possible date. It is argued that this would allow time for her brother and sister-in-law to travel from the States to England. Given Warren Plath's letter was dated the 20 February and he describes travelling back from Hebden Bridge on the 19th, it seems most likely that the service took place on the 18 February.

Bibliography

Primary Plath texts

Plath, Sylvia, 1962. 'Context'. *The London Magazine* New Series 1. 45-46. February.

Plath, Sylvia, 1977. *Johnny Panic and the Bible of Dreams*. London: Faber & Faber.

Plath, Sylvia, 1981. *Collected Poems*. London: Faber & Faber.

Plath, Sylvia, 1982. *The Collected Poems*. (ed.), Ted Hughes. New York: Harper & Row.

Plath, Sylvia, 1982. *The Journals of Sylvia Plath*. New York: Ballantine Books.

Plath, Sylvia, 1986. *The Bell Jar*. First published 1963. London: Faber & Faber.

Plath, Sylvia, 1988. *Letters Home*. Ed. Aurelia Schober Plath. London: Faber & Faber.

Plath, Sylvia, 1990. *Collected Poems*. London: Faber & Faber.

Plath, Sylvia, 2000. *Journals of Sylvia Plath*. (ed.), Karen Kukil. London: Faber & Faber.

Plath, Sylvia, 2004. *Ariel: The Restored Edition*. London: Faber & Faber.

Biographical texts about Sylvia Plath

Alexander, Paul, 1991. *Rough Magic: A Biography of Sylvia Plath*. London: Penguin.

Becker, Jillian, 2003. *Giving Up: The Last Days of Sylvia Plath*. London: Ferrington.

Bronfen, Elisabeth, 1998. *Sylvia Plath*. Plymouth: Northcote House.

Bundtzen, Lynda K., 2001. *The Other Ariel*. Amherst: University of Massachusetts Press.

Butscher, Edward, 1977. *Sylvia Plath: The Woman and the Work*. New York: Dodd, Mead and Company.

Hayman, Ronald, 1991. *The Death and Life of Sylvia Plath*. New York: Birch Lane Press.

Hunter Steiner, Nancy, 1973. *A Closer Look at Ariel: A Memory of Sylvia Plath*. New York: Harper's Magazine Press.

Middlebrook, Diane, 2003. *Her Husband*. London: Viking.

Rollyson, Carl, 2013. *American Isis: The Life and Art of Sylvia Plath*. New York: St Martin's Press.

Steinberg, Peter K., 2004. *Great Writers: Sylvia Plath*. Philadelphia: Chelsea House.

Stevenson, Anne, 1989. *Bitter Fame*. London: Viking.

Thomas, Trevor, 1989. *Last Encounters: A memoir of Sylvia Plath*. Privately published: Bedford. Author's own copy numbered 131 and signed.

Tyrer, Nicola, 2004. 'Secret Life of Sylvia Plath' in *The Daily Mail*, 5 February.

Wagner-Martin, Linda, 1988a. *Sylvia Plath: A Biography*. London: Chatto & Windus.

Wilson, Andrew, 2013. *Mad Girl's Love Song: Sylvia Plath and Life Before Ted*. London: Simon & Schuster.

General Bibliography

Alvarez, Al, 1971. *The Savage God: A Study of Suicide*. London: Penguin.

Bachelard, Gaston, 1994. (First published 1958). *The Poetics of Space*. Boston: Beacon Press.

Banita, Georgiana, 2007. 'The Same, Identical Woman: Sylvia Plath in the Media.' in *The Journal of the Midwestern Modern Language Association*. Fall, Volume 40, Number 2.

Barthes, Roland, 1977. *Image Music Text*. London: Fontana Press.

Barthes, Roland, 1993. *The Pleasure of the Text*. From *Roland Barthes A*

Reader ed. Susan Sontag. London: Vintage first published 1973.

Britzolakis, Christina, 2000. *Sylvia Plath & The Theatre of Mourning*. Oxford: Oxford University Press.

Bronfen, Elisabeth, 1992. *Over Her Dead Body: death, femininity and the aesthetic*. Manchester: Manchester University Press.

Buse, Peter, 1999. *Ghosts: deconstruction, psychoanalysis and history*. London: Macmillan.

Connors, Kathleen, & Bayley, Sally, 2007. *Eye Rhymes Sylvia Plath's Art of the Visual*. Oxford: Oxford University Press.

Crowther, Gail & Peter K. Steinberg, 2009. 'These Ghostly Archives' in *Plath Profiles* Vol. 2. Summer 2009. Indiana University.

Crowther, Gail & Peter K. Steinberg, 2013. 'These Ghostly Archives 5: Reanimating the Past' in *Plath Profiles* Vol. 6. Summer 2013. Indiana University.

Davies, Colin, 2007. *Haunted Subjects: Deconstruction, Psychoanalysis and the Return of the Dead*. Basingstoke: Palgrave.

Degen, Monica, & Kevin Hetherington, 2001. 'Hauntings' in Hetherington, Kevin (ed.), Spacial Hauntings *Space and Culture* Issue 11/12 December.

Derrida, Jacques, 1989. *Memoires for Paul de Man*. New York: Columbia University Press.

Derrida, Jacques, 2001. *The Work of Mourning*. Chicago & London: University of Chicago Press.

Feinstein, Elaine 2001. *Ted Hughes The Life of a Poet*. London: Weidenfeld and Nicolson.

Freud, Sigmund, [1917]. 'Mourning and Melancholia.' in *The Freud Reader* (ed.), Peter Gay. London: Vintage, 1995.

Freud, Sigmund, [1919]. 'The Uncanny.' [online] Available at http://people.emich.edu/acoykenda/uncanny1.html [Accessed 11 December 2008].

Gordon, Avery, 1997. *Ghostly Matters: haunting and the sociological imagination*. Minneapolis: University of Minnesota.

Hallam, Elizabeth, & Jenny Hockey, 2001. *Death, Memory and Material Culture*. Oxford, New York: Berg.

Helle, Anita, 2007. *The Unravelling Archive*. Ann Arbour: University of Michigan.

Hetherington, Kevin, 2001. 'Phantasmagoria/Phantasm Agora: Materialities, Spacialities and Ghosts' Spacial Hauntings *Space and Culture* Issue 11/12 December.

Hockey, Jenny, et al., 2001. *Grief, Mourning and Death Ritual.* Buckingham: Open University Press.

Hughes, Gerald, 2012. *Ted and I.* London: The Robson Press.

Hughes, Olwyn, 1990. 'The Plath Myth and the Reviewing of *Bitter Fame*' in *Poetry Review* Volume 80 No 3. Autumn 1990.

Hughes, Ted, 1989. Letter to *The Independent* newspaper, April.

Hughes, Ted, 1998. *Birthday Letters.* London: Faber & Faber.

Hughes, Ted, 2007. *The Collected Letters of Ted Hughes.* (ed.), Christopher Reid London: Faber & Faber.

Kendall, Tim, 2001. *Sylvia Plath A Critical Study.* London: Faber & Faber.

Malcolm, Janet, 1994. *The Silent Woman.* New York: Alfred A Knopf.

Miles, Michael, 2001. 'Ghostly Pasts, Spectral Futures.' in Hetherington, Kevin Ed. Spacial Hauntings *Space and Culture* Issue 11/12 December.

Moses, Kate, 2003. *Wintering.* New York: St Martin's.

Newman, Charles, 1970. *The Art of Sylvia Plath: A Symposium.* London: Faber & Faber.

Orr, Peter, 1966. *The Poet Speaks: Interviews with Contemporary Poets Conducted by Hilary Morrish, Peter Orr, John Press and Ian Scott-Kilvert.* London: Routledge & K. Paul. [online] Available at http://www.sylviaplath.de/plath/orrinterview.html [Accessed 3 May 2010]

Reader, Ian, & Tony Walter, 1993. *Pilgrimage in Popular Culture.* Basingstoke, Hampshire: Palgrave.

Rose, Jacqueline, 1991. *The Haunting of Sylvia Plath.* London: Virago.

Samuel, Raphael, 1994. *Theatres of Memory.* London: Verso.

Steedman, Carolyn, 2001. *Dust.* Manchester: Manchester University Press.

Thurschwell, Pamela, 2000. *Sigmund Freud.* London: Routledge.

Trinidad, David, 2010. 'Hidden in Plain Sight' in *Plath Profiles* Vol. 3. Summer 2010. Indiana University.

Wagner, Erica, 2000. *Ariel's Gift.* London: Faber & Faber.

Wagner Martin, Linda, 1988b. *Sylvia Plath The Critical Heritage.* London: Routledge.

Wilson, Frances, 1999. *Literary Seductions: Compulsive Writers and Diverted Readers.* London: Faber and Faber.

Winter, Jay, 1998. *Sites of Memory, Sites of Mourning.* Cambridge: Canto Press.

Wolfreys, Julian, 2002. *Victorian hauntings: Spectrality, Gothic, the uncanny & Literature*. Basingstoke: Palgrave.

Yeats, W. B., 1953. *The Collected Plays of W. B. Yeats*. London: MacMillan and Co.

Young, Robert, 1987. *Untying the Text*. London: Routledge.

Young-Bruehl, Elisabeth, 1998. *Subject to Biography: Psychoanalysis, Feminism and Writing Women's Lives*. Cambridge and London: Harvard University Press.

Illustrations

All photographs are copyrighted to the author, Gail Crowther, with the exception of Court Green copyright Peter K. Steinberg, Furniture at Smith College copyright Karen V. Kukil, Mortimer Rare Book Room, Smith College. All images must not be reproduced without permission.